36 Tools for Building Spirit
in *Learning Communities*

*This book is dedicated to all educators who work
tirelessly to build spirit in learning communities.*

36 Tools for Building Spirit in *Learning Communities*

R. Bruce Williams

CORWIN PRESS
A SAGE Publications Company
Thousand Oaks, California

For information:

Corwin Press
A Sage Publications Company
2455 Teller Road
Thousand Oaks, California 91320
www.corwinpress.com

Sage Publications Ltd.
1 Oliver's Yard
55 City Road
London EC1Y 1SP
United Kingdom

Sage Publications India Pvt. Ltd.
B-42, Panchsheel Enclave
Post Box 4109
New Delhi 110 017 India

Printed in the United States of America

Library of Congress Cataloging-in-Publication Data

Williams, R. Bruce.
36 tools for building spirit in learning communities / by R. Bruce Williams.
    p. cm.
Includes bibliographical references and index.
ISBN 1-4129-1344-6 (cloth: acid-free paper)
ISBN 1-4129-1345-4 (pbk.: acid-free paper)
  1. School management and organization. 2. School improvement programs.
3. Teacher participation in administration. I. Title: Thirty-six tools for building spirit in learning communities. II. Title.
LB2805.W522 2006
371.2—dc22

2005035812

This book is printed on acid-free paper.

06 07 08 09 10 9 8 7 6 5 4 3 2 1

Acquisitions Editor:	Jean Ward
Editorial Assistant:	Jordan Barbakow
Production Editor:	Denise Santoyo
Typesetter:	C&M Digitals (P) Ltd.
Indexer:	Pam Van Huss
Cover Designer:	Lisa Miller

Contents

List of Tables and Figures

Templates

Preface

ABOUT THIS BOOK ■

I invite you to go right to the chapter in this book that interests you most. This book does not need to be read sequentially from page 1 to the end. Perhaps a chapter introduction intrigues you. Perhaps your attention goes immediately to a particular activity.

The book describes seven areas, each discussed in a separate chapter, that contribute to spirit in learning communities. To carry out the intent to build or to increase school morale, it is important to have something going on in each of these seven areas; rather than choosing just one of the areas and pursuing several of its activities, it is more effective to implement one or two activities in each of the seven areas.

I would welcome hearing how any part of this book has helped you. In addition, I would love to hear how you have modified something in the book to make it work for you.

ACKNOWLEDGMENTS ■

This book has come about in great measure because of the strong encouragement of Corwin Press Acquisitions Editor Jean Ward. Her guidance and support greatly enabled the writing.

This book owes a huge debt of gratitude to Jack Wallace, my life partner, who spent weeks of effort editing the book and creating the professional-looking graphics, figures, and tables that appear throughout the book.

In addition, Corwin Press gratefully acknowledges the contributions of the following reviewers:

Pamela K. Van Mooy
Elementary Principal
Field Elementary School,
    Fostoria, OH

Nancy Rottenecker
Subschool Principal, High School
    Administrator
Fairfax County, VA

Nicolette Carrell Dennis
Highland Cluster Leader Principal
Bandelier Elementary School
    Principal
Albuquerque Public Schools,
Albuquerque, NM

Arlene C. Miguel
Elementary Principal
Hampden Meadows School,
   Barrington, RI

John Kito
William Tyson Elementary
   School Principal
Anchorage, AK

Cynthia Gudowski Luna
2004 National Distinguished Principal
Educator
San Antonio, TX

Sharon Brittingham
Adjunct Professor and Retired Principal
Educator
Selbyville, DE

About the Author

 **R. Bruce Williams** has more than 35 years of international consulting experience, and is noted for his expert group facilitation and his skills in planning and team building methodologies. He has authored *More Than 50 Ways to Build Team Consensus* (1993) and *Twelve Roles of Facilitators for School Change* (1997). He is also the coauthor of *Valuing Diversity in the School System* (1995) and *Brain-Compatible Learning for the Block* (1997). Recently released are his books *Cooperative Learning: A Standard for High Achievement* (2002), *Multiple Intelligences for Differentiated Learning* (2002), and *Higher Order Thinking Skills: Challenging All Students to Achieve* (2003). His specialty is facilitating participative, interactive group workshops whether these are focused on strategic planning and consensus building or on instructional methodologies for the classroom. Recently, his workshops on Brain-Compatible Learning and School Change Facilitation have been popular. In addition, he frequently presents in the areas of cooperative learning, higher-order thinking skills, and authentic assessment.

Williams brings exceptional skills for dealing with diverse populations, aided by his seven years of experience in Japan and Korea teaching English as a second language. His 36 years of experience in adult training have made him an invaluable resource in facilitating school change.

In addition to conference workshops in 2002 in Australia and New Zealand, he has been invited three times in the last two years to present workshops for teachers in Singapore. In April of 2004, he was the keynote speaker for 400 principals and teachers in Beijing, People's Republic of China.

Introduction

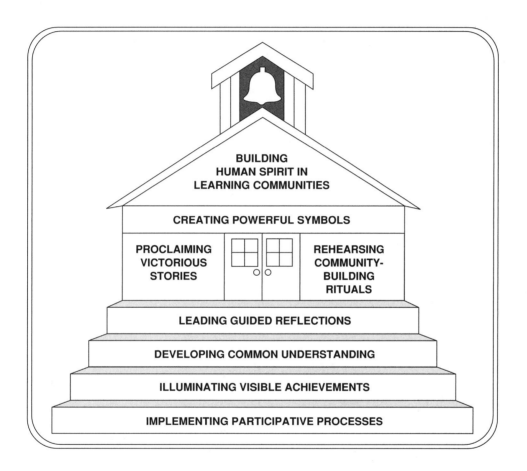

Knitting the elements of culture into an artistic tapestry is like creating a word from the letters of the alphabet. Juxtaposed with one another the letters form a meaningful expression, just as combining the elements of culture create[s] a cohesive school identity.

— Terrence E. Deal and Kent Peterson, 1999,
Shaping School Culture (p. 69)

An elementary school had a faculty that worked well together for many years. When a new elementary school opened in the district, several of this school's faculty were reassigned to teach at the new school. The remaining faculty seemed to be in shock. Certainly, they had lost a lot of their motivation. At the beginning of a strategic planning and implementation workshop, the mood was heavy. Participation was labored at first. As people began to talk together, listen to each other's continued hopes for their school, and make plans for the future, the climate changed. One sign of that was the active participation of a person everyone reported never talked out loud in meetings.

As a result of their planning, school teams were created that continued to meet regularly to implement the plans they had made. The principal met faithfully with the teams to encourage their work. A coordinating team met regularly to make sure that teams were on target with their plans. As the year progressed, their morale rose sharply and successes replaced their original mood of despair with one of hope and inspiration.

Some of the factors that contributed to this turnaround in morale were the participation of the entire faculty in planning and implementation, the targeting and accomplishment of visible achievements, the common understanding that arose out of the planning time together, and the bonding power of the reflective conversations held during the planning time. In addition, the principal continually used her symbolic power in positive and supportive ways.

■ PURPOSE OF THIS BOOK

School change is complicated. Many books have given many clues on how to affect change in a school. These have offered significant clues for encouraging and enhancing school change. This book shares tools and experiences to help school leaders impact the school culture and build spirit across the whole school's community of learners. These tools are specifically designed to help raise morale and build spirit. It goes without saying that teachers can use many of these tools in their classrooms.

This book may be read cover to cover or explored wherever interest leads the reader. It encourages the reader to discover where particular interests are and then delve into that part of the book.

■ OUR TIMES

Reforming and recreating schools is a major theme of our times. "Reforms that bring new technologies or higher standards won't succeed without being embedded in supportive, spirit-filled cultures. Schools won't become what students deserve until cultural patterns and ways are shaped to support learning" (Deal & Peterson, 1999, p. 137). Some of the directions for reform proposed today seem to focus on external solutions. Policies and mandates are imposed from the outside. More assessments are proposed (Deal & Peterson, 1999, pp. xi–xii).

The purpose of this book is not to suggest that any of these external solutions are mistaken. Rather, it is to offer that taken alone these external solutions will not work, because no real improvement can occur without significant support from within the school culture. Furthermore, for Deal and Peterson (1999, p. xii) the school culture is integral for increasing student learning and achievement.

In the midst of these challenging times, it is tempting to offer clear-cut answers; that is not the purpose of this book. Hopefully, this book shines some light on areas that assist our work in schools such as increasing levels of participation in the school community, creating common understandings of what the school hopes to accomplish, implementing visible achievements, and expanding the power of stories, rituals, and symbols. "We need new strategies to work within a world where strangeness becomes stranger over time and where no explanation maintains its usefulness for long" (Eoyang, 1997, p. 3). Unless we focus attention on enlivening the spirit and on awakening morale, no amount of reform or mandate or policy or assessment will totally solve the challenges we face today in education. Education once again needs to be a source of inspiration, motivation, and aspiration.

OUR CHALLENGE ■

To balance the huge effort of focusing on the externals—that is outcomes, mandates, and assessments—there needs to be a focus on the internal (Deal & Peterson, 1999, p. xi). The world is changing fast. Our students are different from students of even 15 or 20 years ago. Technology has leaped forward, and many students have made the leap. Diversity has transformed the makeup of our schools. Often the change has happened so fast that schools are trying to figure out how to best respond. In many ways the institutional structure of many of our educational facilities has become dreadfully outdated.

The challenge education faces in the midst of increasing external pressure and accountability is to look deep within the entire school system—indeed, the entire school culture—and deal with those forces that allow negativity, fragmentation, and despair to fester. Senge (1990) is helpful for us here:

> The systems perspective tells us that we must look beyond individual mistakes or bad luck to understand important problems. We must look beyond personalities and events. We must look into the underlying structures which shape individual actions and create the conditions where types of events become likely. (pp. 42–43)

The issue is not people; that is, it is not the teachers nor the students nor the administration. The issue is not the curriculum. The issue is not even the external mandates and pushes for accountability. The issue is not leadership style or method of decision making. And yet all of these are important and need to be addressed in every school. The issue is what lies underneath all of that in the makeup of the school culture.

Fortunately, there are ways to discern what the underlying environment and culture are. Furthermore, much can be done to transform negativity, fragmentation, and despair.

> The reason that structural explanations are so important is that only they address the underlying causes of behavior at a level that

patterns of behavior can be changed. Structure produces behavior, and changing underlying structures can produce different patterns of behavior. In this sense, structural explanations are inherently generative. Moreover, since structure in human systems includes the "operating policies" of the decision makers in the system, redesigning our own decision making redesigns the system structure. (Senge, 1990, p. 53)

A focus on the underlying school culture can actually alter patterns of behavior. Consequently, unlike the difficulty of meeting external mandates and new forms of accountability, the faculty and the administration can totally control many aspects of the school culture. The tools that can enable impacting the school culture are at the heart of this book. Deal and Peterson (1999, p. 127) remind us that this is no easy task. Nevertheless, it is a possible task, because the human beings that make up the culture and the structures of a school are right there in the school.

The nature of structure in human systems is subtle because we are part of the structure. This means that we often have the power to alter structures within which we are operating. However, more often than not, we do not perceive that power. (Senge, 1990, p. 44)

When appropriate time and attention are given to the school environment and culture, the impossible and overwhelming become possible and manageable. This can happen because a new perspective is born. A new energy is tapped.

■ A WORD ABOUT CULTURE

What is it that we are calling culture or, in our case, school culture? As we said earlier, it is invisible—yet its manifestations are very visible and palpable in a school. The culture of a school is sensed immediately upon entering the school.

"We believe the term *culture* provides a more accurate and intuitively appealing way to help school leaders better understand their school's own unwritten rules and traditions, norms, and expectations that seem to permeate everything" (Deal & Peterson, 1999, p. 2).

The key in what Deal and Peterson are suggesting is that whatever we are referring to with the term *culture* is omnipresent. It is underneath and behind all that goes on in the life of a school. It is the real source of the "unwritten rules and traditions, norms, and expectations." This is why it needs attention. Left uncared for it can evolve into that which breeds negativity, fragmentation, and despair. It is culture that underlies all that goes on in school and directly affects beliefs as well as teacher and student behaviors (Deal & Peterson, 1999, p. 3).

School culture forms the beliefs and behaviors of the school's everyday life. No matter what external rules and expectations are prevalent, unless culture is transformed, little that is positive and affirming can survive. The underlying culture impacts how teachers, students, staff, support personnel think, act, and feel as they work day in and day out in the school (Deal & Peterson, 1999, p. 4).

Toxic Cultures

Deal and Peterson (1999) analyzed the presence of "toxic cultures"; their thinking on this is organized into chart form in Table 0.1.

Four primary characteristics of toxic cultures stand out. The first is the prevalence of negative values. This does not mean that a school never talks about or deals with negative issues. It does mean that the danger is that negative values and beliefs become the predominant ones. When negative issues overwhelm the possibility of any solution, the possibility of toxic culture dramatically increases.

Fragmentation refers to the divisions among faculty and staff that have become more operational than the whole community. Not all smaller groups are unhelpful. Notice that the key concern is with the smaller groups that have become negative in their influence.

The third characteristic of toxic cultures is the presence of destructive acts. It is one thing for people to keep negative values and beliefs to themselves. It is even different if they are only talked about. Toxic cultures arise with intentional acts whose purpose, conscious or unconscious, is out to tear down.

The final characteristic is fractured spirit. When spirit is fractured, there is little positive underlying glue holding the school community together. That is, people—teachers, students, and administrators—are just going through the motions.

These characteristics show up concretely in the life of the school. When a focus on negative values shows up, negative values are in total control. This shows up in people who find it impossible to imagine a positive outcome. This shows up in people who have lost their vision of what

Table 0.1   Toxic Cultures

Characteristics	Elements	Antidotes
Prevalence of negative values	Control by negative values and beliefs	Confront head on.
Fragmentation	Negative groups and cliques	Support positive cultural elements and subgroups.
Destructive acts	Negative roles: Saboteurs Pessimists Prima donnas Deadwood Martyrs	Recruit, select, and retain effective positive staff.
Fractured spirit	Meaningless rituals and traditions	Create new stories of success, renewal, and accomplishment.

Adapted from Deal, T. E., & Peterson, K. (1999). *Shaping school culture* (pp. 118–129). San Francisco: Jossey-Bass.

education and school can be. This shows up in people who are only out for the paycheck or the good grade.

Fragmentation shows up with the presence of a myriad of strong, overpowering small groups or cliques. Cliques that are really out to foster positive growth and achievement in the life of a school are valuable. Such cliques put the good of the whole school ahead of their own specific hopes and agendas. Cliques that only support their own agendas result in a harmful fragmentation that ends up frustrating the well-meaning efforts of positive groups.

There are individuals and groups who move beyond negative beliefs to concrete, specific destructive acts. They not only disagree but are out to derail any healthy and positive direction. These can be the overt saboteurs, the negative storytellers, those who only want the spotlight, and those who depend on others to pull the weight.

Finally, the fractured spirit manifests itself in lifeless school community events. Over and over again, people carry out just more of the same. An event occurs only because it has happened every year for the last 50 years. The energy that created the tradition or the event in the first place has long since past. Another manifestation of the fractured spirit is the burned-out teacher or student. The pressure has become overwhelming. Life has been snuffed out.

The antidotes are very much on target. They are excellent antidotes regardless of the characteristic or element a school is dealing with. It is up to the school leaders to decide which antidote best meets the needs of a particular situation.

The first antidote is to confront negative values and beliefs head on. Without naming people, it is still possible to name the negative value and belief and to describe how it shows up. One can offer alternative positive values and beliefs that will characterize the school's culture from then on. This can be done forcefully and does not need to convey judgment of individuals.

Another effective antidote is to spend the bulk of available energy supporting those individuals and groups who embody constructive positive beliefs and actions. Instead of battling the negative forces, strengthen the positive ones and watch what happens. As positive victories amass, the negative will be forced to retreat.

A related antidote has to do with bringing more and more constructive and positive staff on board. The flip side, of course, is to encourage the negative, destructive staff to find other places of employment. Sometimes that can be the most helpful strategy for helping them change. The presence of new people will energize those faithful, positive staff members who have been working so hard to bring success and improvement.

Finally, the last antidote is one that much space in this book is used to develop. Briefly, it involves creating and highlighting great new stories of what is working and what is bringing about success. Stories and artifacts that demonstrate victories do wonders to unify the spirit of the entire school community. They help to remind everyone why they chose to become educators in the first place, remind the community why school is such an essential part of any community, and communicate success to students and the community.

A WORD ABOUT SPIRIT ■

My intent in these following sections is to demystify this word *spirit* and thereby make it a more approachable word. It is a word that needs to be recovered if we are to bring life into our educational institutions.

Culture and Spirit

Harrison Owen says

"Culture is the dynamic field within which Spirit is shaped, formed and directed" (Owen, 1987, p. 121).

"Culture is the dynamic field within which the spirit of man assumes its shape and gets its job done" (Adams, 1986, p. 115).

The previous section talked about culture and its role in setting the tone, the milieu, the atmosphere of a school. Owen's words liken culture to a "dynamic field." It is this dynamic field that allows spirit to operate, to grow, to form, and to work. From this it becomes apparent that culture invites, forms, and encourages the presence of spirit. As indicated previously, toxic cultures diminish or extinguish spirit. Healthy cultures encourage and feed spirit. When that happens, the spirit can attend to its task of enlivening and deepening the human enterprise.

In the powerful, well-formed cultures, the spirit is strong, and tasks are accomplished with dispatch. But when the culture (dynamic field) becomes weak, flaccid, and incoherent, the spirit loses its intention and direction. So if our intention is to ensure that the spirit of a particular organization is adequate to the task at hand, and to those tasks that may lie just over the horizon, our area of operation will be the culture of the organization. (Adams, 1986, p. 115)

For Owen, when one is concerned about spirit in an organization, one needs to focus on the organization's culture. Only by turning one's attention to the culture can one revive the spirit. It would seem from this that more specific job descriptions, stronger accountability, even good skills training (all of which are needed and important) will not complete the job without also strengthening the healthy culture of an organization. How does one begin? Where does a school team start? According to Allen and Kraft, "The cultural approach means looking beyond individual causes and solutions to the social factors that influence us and to make use of those factors to create change" (Adams, 1984, p. 37). Looking at the culture means looking at the pieces that make up the culture—its social interactions; its knowledge and beliefs; its style of operating, its stories, formal and informal; its ceremonies and rites; and its key visual symbols.

Spirit as Energy, Force, and Vitality

One can find spirit everywhere, in all individuals and in all groups and organizations. Bolman and Deal (1995, p. 20) suggest that spirit is the "internal force that sustains meaning and hope." James A. Ritscher writes, "The spirit of an organization is its heart, its vital nature. Spirit is a sense of vitality, energy, vision, and purpose. All organizations have spirit, but in some cases it is dull and tarnished" (Adams, 1986, p. 62). Perhaps we begin to get a glimpse of what these writers are talking about when we recall comments like, "That was a spirited discussion we had this morning." In that context we might be talking about a lively discussion, a vibrant discussion, a discussion with much vitality. Whatever force creates a sense of drive, energy, and aliveness is the force these writers are pointing to with the word *spirit*.

Owen reminds us that spirit has often been connected with breath or wind. In this way spirit is "that vital energy or force that underlies all physical reality." Likewise, then, the underlying reality of all organizations is "spirit and flow." If this is true, then one can easily ascertain that the task of school leadership teams is to "focus the spirit and enhance its power," and direct the flow and spirit toward the attainment of the school's mission and objectives (Adams, 1986, p. 113).

While we have avoided using words like spirit and spirituality in the context of education, it is time to see that unless we find appropriate ways to understand these dynamics, learning communities will become lifeless and devoid of values. Without discovering appropriate ways to bring spirit back into educational institutions, administrators, teachers, and students will continue to lose motivation and hope. "Spirit and faith are the core of human life. Without them, you lose your way. You live without zest. You go through the motions, but there's no passion" (Bolman & Deal, 1995, p. 20). When this happens, administration, teachers, and students become meaningless to each other. Everyone begins to feel they are playing an inauthentic game. With spirit present, on the other hand, school becomes an exciting place to work and to learn. With spirit present, school becomes a place of hope for all.

Spirit Versus Religion

There is obviously a danger when bringing such words as spirit and soul into this book about education and schools. Public schools have been established to be free of a specific religion, doctrine, church, temple, or mosque. People are rightfully distressed when those boundaries are crossed in public education.

Ritscher comes to the rescue here with helpful clarity:

When I use the word spiritual, I am not referring to religion. A religion is an organization that professes to provide spiritual experiences to groups of people. Spirituality, however, is more an individual matter; it does not rely on an external organization. Rather, spirituality is an experience of depth in life; it is living life with heart rather than superficiality. For some, spirituality involves the belief in a god. For others, it takes a different form. In any case, spirituality is the awareness that there is something more to life than just our narrow, ego-oriented view of it. (Adams, 1986, p. 61)

Strengthening the spirit has to do with experiencing the depth in life, going beneath surface realities to heartfelt core realities. Howard Gardner lately has talked a great deal about enabling schools to help students discern "the true, the beautiful, and the good" (Gardner, 2000, p. 143). This is all distinct from any religious doctrine or religious institutions. Yet in our fear of trespassing, often education has steered away from any of the above. When we do that, we rob our students of the opportunity to explore their own depths and to develop their own strong spirits. When we do that, we are abdicating to the loudest commercial market forces to shape our students' depths. "What has escaped us is a deep understanding of the spirit, purpose, and meaning of the human experience" (Bolman & Deal, 1995, p. 8).

Feeding the Spirit

As with any living thing, without nourishment, without encourage-ment the human spirit withers, goes dormant, or perhaps even dies. So one of our challenges is how to feed the human spirit, how to help it grow into health and strength. In their book *Leading with Soul*, Bolman and Deal say the spirit is fed by offering people "gifts from the heart," which inculcate meaning, depth, and passion (1995, p. 12).

If our schools can't do this, if our leaders can't bring spirit to life, then we will find our schools faltering under the pressure of this trend and that fad (Adams, 1986, p. 62). Only schools strong in spirit will have the drive and strength to transform themselves into schools meeting the needs of this twenty-first century. The spirit resources are plentiful in our schools. These resources only need attention and focus. Owen (1987) challenges us here: "Dealing with Spirit is not just nice, it is essential. For Spirit may be the only thing we have left" (p. 2).

STRUCTURE OF EACH ACTIVITY ◼

At the end of the chapters in this book are activities, each of which begins with a general description of what the activity is and continues with a step-by-step outline of the method for carrying out the activity. An example follows to clarify exactly how the activity can be used. Finally, the activity concludes with a "metacognitive insight." Metacognitive here means a reflective or deeper interpretation of the activity itself. Often addi-tional hints are given to enable the practitioner to carry out the activity successfully.

TEMPLATES ◼

Many of the activities use a form to help guide the practitioner. This form is often found in the examples filled out as one might use it. In the back of the book, blanks of many of these forms are included. It is the hope that practitioners will find these blanks useful in implementing these activities in their schools.

1

Implementing Participative Processes

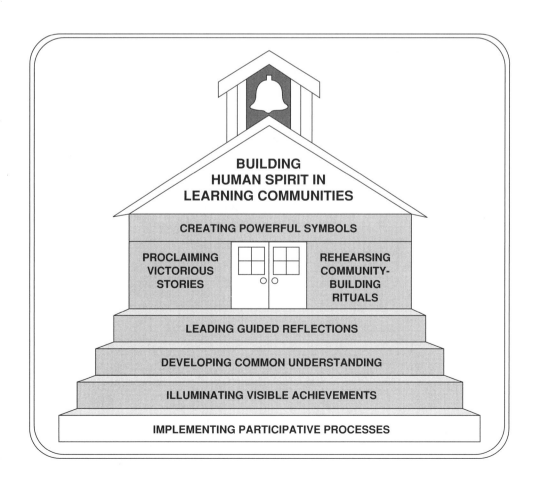

BUILDING
HUMAN SPIRIT IN
LEARNING COMMUNITIES

CREATING POWERFUL SYMBOLS

PROCLAIMING
VICTORIOUS
STORIES

REHEARSING
COMMUNITY-
BUILDING
RITUALS

LEADING GUIDED REFLECTIONS

DEVELOPING COMMON UNDERSTANDING

ILLUMINATING VISIBLE ACHIEVEMENTS

IMPLEMENTING PARTICIPATIVE PROCESSES

Participation, though, is not an isolated phenomenon. It is part of a wider circle of factors that define how human beings relate to one another in our times. It is a key component of the new paradigm of living in the 21st century, and as such, finds allies in other kindred disciplines such as conflict mediation, dispute partnering, and facilitative leadership, to name a few.

—James P. Troxel, 1993, *Participation Works: Business Cases from Around the World* (p. 6)

A new principal at a middle school discerned quickly that his faculty was fragmented and in some disarray. He asked a facilitator to help his faculty pull together a practical vision that they could all buy into. This facilitator spent a day with the faculty and left them with a vision of where they wanted to be in three years as well as structured implementation teams to get them there. The workshop methods used drew totally on the full participation of everyone there. All left feeling their voice had been heard.

A couple of years later when he was transferred to another middle school, he called this facilitator back to do a similar workshop with his faculty. And a year later when he took over as a high school principal, once again he wanted to unite his staff with the participatory methods to fashion a vision and implementation plan.

For him the key was the participation and consensus that emerged in each situation. In addition, what encouraged further participation after the workshop were the realistic visible achievements each faculty created and implemented. In every one of these schools, these achievements strengthened the staff's conviction that theirs was a school parents were proud to have their children attend. Furthermore, the principal as leader fostered the kind of atmosphere that called for excellence in achievement.

The paradigm has shifted. A century ago most people were satisfied to follow and to take orders. Top-down decision making worked. In these last decades it has become clear that no one person can hold all the data and embody all the perspectives needed to make clear and wise decisions. Hence we come upon the need for participative processes.

■ THE DRIVE FOR COLLABORATION

Human beings have a very natural capacity for working and thinking together.

> [David] Bohm had shared with me in London an explicit mental model of the way he believed the world works and the way he believed human beings learn and think. To Bohm it was clear that humans have an innate capacity for collective intelligence. They can learn and think together, and this collaborative thought can lead to coordinated action. (Jaworski, 1996, p. 109)

As we look around the world, we can see evidence of this capacity even more clearly in certain cultures that seem to operate much more collaboratively than Western cultures. Somehow it got through to human beings that thinking and working together could better solve some problems.

In addition, there are other facts that need to be highlighted here:

> In the personal sense, however, a collaborative life is much more satisfying. Synergy is the reason. Our collective energy is greater than the sum of our individual energies. In the professional sense, what we can accomplish is immeasurably greater. (Joyce & Showers, 1995, p. 39)

The first fact mentioned is that collaboration can be much more satisfying. When done well, energy emerges. This is often referred to as *synergy*, and it can be extremely rewarding and motivating. The second fact is that the energy in successful collaboration is much stronger than even the total of the individual energies. Because this energy can feed motivation, there is potential for much greater accomplishment.

The heart of this drive, this capacity for collaboration is a human being's ability to empathize, to see common themes, common struggles in other people. It would seem, then, that this ability for empathy is a natural one in human beings. Kohn (1990, p. 163) summarizes this: "Whether or not empathy is seen as natural—or more natural than its absence—a case can be made that it is a human capacity that will flourish unless some force interferes with its development and actualization."

If all of the above is true, then the implications for education are compelling. So much of an educator's life occurs in relative isolation. The classroom teacher is often isolated from teacher colleagues. Brief encounters in the lunchroom or teachers' lounge do little to counteract the far longer periods of teaching alone or planning alone. "Giving up isolation is probably the area that causes the greatest concern in the process of developing a collaborative school. We find that we *liked* autonomy. Thrashing out collective decisions is much more complicated at first" (Joyce & Showers, 1995, p. 39). Whether teachers have liked autonomy or autonomy has been forced upon them, there will need to be dramatic changes in the traditional ways teachers have related to each other as well as the ways teachers and administrators have related to each other (Joyce & Showers, 1995, p. 38). The bottom line, finally, is that teachers "could improve considerably if they were in a more collaborative environment" (Fullan & Hargreaves, 1996, p. 10).

This leads us to the necessity of creating a culture of participation. This leads us to face the reality that today's climate is one of effective participation.

THE EMERGENCE OF ◼
A PARTICIPATIVE CULTURE

The 20th century saw the rise of a culture of participation. A century ago, decisions were made by people at the top and filtered down to the people involved. Most people waited to be told what to do and then did it. Almost anyone in a leadership position today will tell you that the autocratic, top-down mode of organizational management doesn't work today. In varying ways and using a multitude of approaches, organizations are turning more and more to some form of participatory involvement for planning and implementing their goals and tasks.

> Participation, though, is not an isolated phenomenon. It is part of a wider circle of factors that define how human beings relate to one another in our times. It is a key component of the new paradigm of living in the 21st century, and as such, finds allies in other kindred disciplines such as conflict mediation, dispute partnering, and facilitative leadership, to name a few. (Troxel, 1993, p. 6)

In other words, there has been a shift in terms of how people relate to each other. Talk to any parent who has discovered children need more than, "Do it because I said so." Talk to any teacher who finds students need to know why they are to do something. This participative culture is part of a lot of other shifts that are marking the age we are living in.

> Be it in the poorest village or plush company office, the cry to be part of the solution and not merely a victim of circumstances has become one of the defining characteristics of life in our time. As such, participation is not simply a luxury that only some people can afford. It is much more—a basic right of every citizen of the globe today. (Troxel, 1993, p. 13)

One of the characteristics of our time is that people are moving away from being victims and are demanding to be a part of some solutions. This is a dramatic shift representing a belief that something can be done. Furthermore, it is a belief that collaborative effort can achieve what individual effort may not be able to accomplish.

> Another large and growing advocacy group for participation has been educators from around the world who cry for more effective, more relevant, and more holistic education. Almost all reform proposals have included some component of increased participation on the part of parents, teachers, administrators, and students in the total education process. (Troxel, 1993, pp. 11–12)

Education has also been touched by this growing move toward participation. Clearly this is obvious with the trends in the last 15 years toward site-based management and shared decision making. Furthermore, the task of creating effective schools has become far more complex than what one person can manage or get one's mind around.

Also, people support more fervently that which they have helped to fashion and put together. "Simply put, not only do employees not fully implement someone's plans, they support more enthusiastically what they themselves create. This is simply part of the new common sense of organizational life today" (Troxel, 1993, p. 24).

> A consultant worked with the faculty of a Midwestern school to create a strategic plan and implementation scheme. After two days of heavy participation, implementation teams had been created. Returning after six months for a half-day check in follow-up, the teams had many successes to report. Several years later this consultant met the principal at a national conference. He reported that teams were still working and implementing projects. Participation blossomed and really became established in this school. Furthermore, the principal supported and encouraged the teams.

Margaret Wheatley (1992) backs this up in the following two statements:

First, I no longer believe that organizations can be changed by imposing a model developed elsewhere. Second, and much more important, the new physics cogently explains that there is no objective reality out there waiting to reveal its secrets. There are no recipes or formulae, no checklists or advice that describe 'reality.' There is only what we create through our engagement with others and with events. (p. 7)

This is both bad news and good news. There are no clear-cut answers and guidelines. Nevertheless, working together, directions and ways to move can be found. Because of this, it is absolutely essential to involve as much wisdom and as many perspectives as possible. "The answer, I believe, is found in the participative nature of the universe. Participation, seriously done, is a way out from the uncertainties and ghostly qualities of this nonobjective world we live in. We need a broad distribution of information, viewpoints, and interpretation if we are to make sense of the world" (Wheatley, 1992, p. 64).

It can't be stressed enough what a change has occurred with this new reality. It means as dramatic a shift as looking at relationships vertically—that is, who is above and below me in society—versus looking at relationships horizontally—that is looking across and around rather than up and down. Because of this, there is no one passing down answers from above. What answers there will be are answers we create. This is the new reality we are now part of. What are the implications of all this? Is this good? How do we operate in this new reality?

THE BENEFITS OF PARTICIPATION ■

"The concept of employee participation has taken hold so firmly that it is hard to find a current book about management that doesn't either promote participation or assume it. Given the trends in the marketplace and the workforce, participation is widely acknowledged as the way of the future. The benefits ascribed to it are numerous" (Spencer, 1989, p. 11).

I would like to highlight several of these benefits. Four crucial ones are buy-in, synergy, team accomplishments, and security/satisfaction.

Buy-in points to what happens when people work together to plan or create something. Because their thinking and sweat went into its creation, it belongs to them. Therefore, there is great buy-in. Synergy points to the development of an energy that occurs when people work well together. This energy can drive the accomplishment of whatever the group's goals are. Team accomplishments point to the greater complexity that can be accomplished when a team works on something versus just one person. Finally, security/satisfaction points to the internal response inside people when they have a chance to work well together. There is a sense of safety and security because more than one person has poured energy into the creation of something. That reduces the anxiety that often occurs when one person ventures out alone to suggest or create something. Satisfaction points to the testimonies of how much more satisfying teamwork and genuine participation are. It satisfies our human need to connect to others in significant ways. "The more all professionals feel part of decision making, the greater their morale, participation, and commitment in carrying out the school's goals" (Gideon & Erlandson, 2001, p. 16). Not only that, some would say that healthy participation can be the crucial factor in whatever needs to be accomplished. "Strengthened participation by all organization members—up and down and sideways on the organizational chart—is the factor that can make the difference" (Blake, Moulton, & Allen, 1987, p. 2). The key to all this is that effective participation can release all of the hidden resources locked in the human potential of a well-functioning team.

Buy-In

Very often school administrators ask, "How do I get my staff on board? How do I get them to buy in to what I want to do?" This raises a huge question. If you want your staff to buy into your ideas 100 percent, they won't. After offering them relevant data, concerns, mandates, educational research, and so forth, they all need to work together to create a winning direction. Then there will be buy-in. "It is far more effective to elicit employee participation in the creation of the vision than to impose the vision on the team. Such input gives team membership a proprietary feeling" (Blake et al., 1987, p. 5). Just as in the classroom, where we know content becomes meaningful to students when they have worked with it themselves, when authentic participation occurs, the opportunity for buy-in increases.

From the perspective of business, Troxel (1993) echoes this:

> Simply put, not only do employees not fully implement someone's plans, they support more enthusiastically what they themselves create. (p. 24)

In one sense, it is much easier to go the top-down route in the short run. The top person issues the decision, and it filters down. However, in this new reality, people balk at mandates and top-down decisions. What is called for is getting people the necessary data, research, and parameters, so that together a satisfactory direction can be created.

Synergy

The energy of a well-functioning team far surpasses that of each individual. "Our collective energy is greater than the sum of our individual energies" (Joyce & Showers, 1995, p. 39). This mysterious energy, which is often observed and felt by sports teams, is what is called synergy. It is as if individual energies bounce off of the energies of other group members creating something entirely different. Fullan and Hargreaves (1996, p. 7) refer to findings in their experience and research, saying, "Collegial schools are powerful forces for change, yet they are also in the minority."

Another way to grasp this synergy is thinking about power. All of this is suggesting that in authentic participation a certain power is released within the team and through the team's accomplishments. In contrasting participation with autocratic leadership, Bolman and Deal (1995, p. 107) concluded that when leaders hoard power, they really create an organization without power. At that point, people one way or another express their anger. However, when power is shared, people gain a sense of effectiveness that helps them feel that their participation makes a difference. The participative processes become a key energy source, a key reservoir of power.

A related fact has to do with trust. When people are trusted, motivation is increased, synergy abounds, and very often better results occur (Bolman & Deal, 1995, p. 106)

Team Accomplishments

This third benefit of participation is the impact magnitude of accomplishments done by a team versus that of many scattered, individual accomplishments. "The key issue is in how the parts act together—participation. It is the core issue of productivity, creativity, and satisfaction" (Blake et al., p. 126). "In the professional sense, what we can accomplish is immeasurably greater" (Joyce & Showers, 1995, p. 39).

Furthermore, if there is to be any impact on the school culture, this can only be accomplished through teams and collaboration. "The reality is that the school climate is developed through collective action" (Joyce & Showers, 1995, p. 28). The reason is that this task of creating and sustaining alive, dynamic schools is too much for one individual to tackle. The world moves quickly. That which is new surrounds education very quickly. Teams have the potential of responding creatively and comprehensively to these challenges. Healthy participation and well-functioning teams both get the job done and have the potential for uplifting and sustaining spirit.

Security/Satisfaction

Teaching is a demanding and front-line job. Many situations a day call for teacher creativity and ingenuity. This creates daily questions of which direction is helpful, which direction is needed. Consequently, ". . . the most important effect of teacher collaboration is its impact on the *uncertainty* of the job, which, when faced alone, can otherwise undermine a teacher's sense of confidence" (Fullan & Hargreaves, 1996, p. 45). The word *security* may be better translated as confidence or assurance in the performing of the teaching task—confidence or assurance in the midst of the tremendous responsibility of impacting the lives of the students in the care of the teacher.

This second dimension is called *satisfaction*. Countless teachers leave the profession each year. Some leave disappointed; some leave angry; some leave beaten; some leave burnt out. "In the personal sense, however, a collaborative life is much more satisfying" (Joyce & Showers, 1995, p. 39). Another benefit of participation and effective teamwork is the potential for high satisfaction that can occur when teams pull off a magnificent accomplishment. When people work well together, their desires for connecting with other adults are satisfied. The bottom line is unless spirit is fed and kept alive, teachers will continue to leave.

Many teachers would be able to bracket their desires for higher external rewards if some intangible benefits were part of their work life. When inner needs are satisfied, when work is challenging but not overwhelming, many work even harder.

> In motivation theory, our attention is shifting from the enticement of external rewards to the intrinsic motivators that spring from the work itself. We are refocusing on the deep longings we have for community, meaning, dignity, and love in our organizational lives. We are beginning to look at the strong emotions that are part of being human, rather than segmenting ourselves. . . . (Wheatley, 1992, p. 12)

■ THE SKILLS FOR PARTICIPATION

Desiring a participative culture does not guarantee it will happen. There are some people who love to be told what to do. There are others who do not want to bear the responsibility of participation. There are people, however, who want their voices heard. There are others who are not satisfied to just hear the orders and do them. No matter what the mixture of people is, participation won't happen unless the leader embodies the skills to encourage participation. Some of these skills are concrete strategies to engender interaction. Others of these skills involve very subtle things like the tone of a voice, the particular use of participation-fostering language.

> Approaches that have increased in popularity have had their day and waned. . . . . None has aimed at strengthening participation by providing members skills of effective behavior essential for participating in a responsible manner; none offers organization members greater insight into the barriers that arise within their team cultures; none say what to do. (Blake et al., 1987, p. 3)

Most of our teachers were trained to go into the classroom and teach. Most of the time, this is done by an individual teacher in a classroom with students but no other adults. Schools are now using teams for a lot of guidance for grade-level, department-level, and whole-school concerns. Many people who become part of such teams are ignorant of the ground rules for successful teamwork. Many are unaware of effective participation methodologies. If we expect administrators and teachers to work in teams, administrators and teachers need to be taught the skills to do that (Byham, 1992, p. ix).

The model of team participation skills includes the following (Blake et al., 1987, pp. 128–129):

Decision making

Objectives

Coordination

Communication

Critique

There are other crucial skills such as listening and paraphrasing. Mirroring the content, the emotions, and the intent of a person's comments can be critical to enabling a team to move forward. Some comment that the use of a flow of individual thinking, team brainstorming, and whole-group discussion has been invaluable. The most important point is that participation does not happen automatically. Participation needs to be nurtured and invited in an open and nonthreatening way.

PEER COACHING   ■

Research is indicating that continuing to carry out training in a relationship of structured, effective collegiality is one way of making the training get into the classroom. "People learn new patterns of behavior primarily through their interactions with others, not through front-end training designs. Training builds on and extends momentum" (Fullan, 1993, p. 68). One helpful way to structure this collegial interaction is through peer coaching. This involves peers having an opportunity to observe each other in their respective classrooms and then providing requested feedback to the peer observed. This observation is not to be confused with supervisory and administrative observations. Nor is this peer observation to be confused with the observation that might go on in a mentor-novice relationship in which the *mentor* teacher is considered more of an expert in the art and skill of teaching. In peer coaching, the relationship is between two equals. Teacher A visits Teacher B's class. Soon after, Teacher B visits Teacher A's class. Consequently, a lateral relationship is built rather than a vertical one.

In no way does peer coaching replace administrative evaluations or mentor programs; rather it expands the opportunities for collegial connection in the school environment. "Effective staff development requires cooperative relationships that break down the isolation and increase the collective strength of the community of educators who staff the school" (Joyce& Showers, 1995, p. 10). The environment of isolation is so prevalent in the educational system that many teachers are either unwilling or fearful to have another adult with them in their classrooms. The very structured approach of peer coaching allows this to happen while maintaining a sense of control in the teacher who is being observed. "Giving up isolation is probably the area that causes the greatest concern in the process of developing a collaborative school. We find we *liked* autonomy. Thrashing out our collective decisions is much more complicated at first. Studying teaching together is more aggravating than deciding how to teach one's own classes with one's best judgment unfettered" (Joyce & Showers, 1995, p. 39). While it is true that a perceived advantage to this isolation is that one gets to run the show on one's own, it is also true that the isolation builds walls among staff that a structure like peer coaching can help to break down. It is one way for the great wisdom of teachers, sometimes developed over a period of years in trying circumstances, can be shared with fellow teachers.

Joyce and Showers (1995) have done substantial research relative to the effectiveness of peer coaching when it is done well. "Designing the workplace so that teachers can work together to implement changes (through peer coaching) is still the key to transferring the content of training into the repertoire of the classroom and school, whether the content is over teaching and curriculum or over processes for collegial action" (p. xv).

Following staff training on peer coaching and a staff decision to proceed with this, staff can pair up into peer coaching teams. The fundamental flow is a preobservation meeting, an observation, and a postobservation meeting. This flow will occur for both of the two peer coaching team members. If team member A is going to visit team member B's class, then the preobservation meeting will offer an opportunity for team member B to state very specifically what team member A will observe during the visit. Team member B will suggest a good time to visit and tell team member A where to sit in the classroom. Team member B may offer some other information on what the curriculum and lesson are focused on and any other material to help team member A to observe. Together they create the data-recording form that team member A will use. Usually the specific item to be observed is something related to a common training each have recently had. Some teachers like their peers to listen carefully to how they give directions and set up an activity. Some teachers want their peers to watch who they call on in class, concerned about gender bias or the well-known T formation (that is, calling exclusively on the front row and the middle row of students). Some teachers want their peers to determine if everyone in cooperative groups is working. The list of things to observe in the classroom is endless. Whatever it is, it is the observed teacher's choice. Finally, the two will decide on a time and place for the postobservation debriefing to occur.

Before the actual observation, teacher B may decide to brief the class on what will occur and to assure them that teacher A is observing her teaching not checking on them. Teacher A then jots down only the data relative to the request. Generally visits can be as short as 20 minutes or so.

During the postobservation debriefing, teacher A may choose to thank teacher B for letting the visit happen. Then teacher A gives the form with the data to teacher B. After teacher B has had a chance to consider the information, teacher A might ask teacher B what the data are indicating. At every point, teacher A is trying to elicit the thinking of teacher B about the data. Then teacher A might ask what some next steps might be. Teacher A makes sure teacher B keeps the data, assuring teacher B that this is all confidential between the two of them. It might now be time to set up the flow for teacher B to visit teacher A's classroom.

The tremendous gift in peer coaching is that it is "a teacher-controlled method for improving instruction that works from within the school and has years of teacher experience to document its success" (Gottesman, 2000, p. 1).

PARTICIPATION DOS AND DON'TS ■

Much can be said about what enables participation and what prevents full participation. The following highlights a few crucial points. If the group cuts across many constituencies, make sure that every constituency is represented. Stated simply, whoever is involved in the issue, concern, or problem needs to participate in creating the solution (Troxel, 1993 p. 24). When participation is the goal, a multitude of perspectives guarantees a rich, comprehensive experience and a product that has a chance to appeal to a broad spectrum within the constituencies. While it may seem simpler to gather only those with similar perspectives, the participation in such a group will be shortchanged. This is especially true if the particular participatory event is a planning process. It is easy to look just within the school walls, at best involving administrators and teachers.

"Planning is a participatory organizational process that involves teachers, parents, students, and administrators in discussing, imagining, and debating desirable alternative states for the immediate and long-term future" (Astuto, Clark, Read, McGree, & Fernandez, 1994, p. 72).

The preceding information emphasizes making sure all the constituencies are involved in participation. A related issue, once the constituencies are there, is using processes that engage and involve everyone who is present. Having excellent representation with diverse perspectives does little good if the processes employed do not fully tap everyone's wisdom in the team or group.

Many of our school communities are becoming more and more diverse as different cultures and different ethnic peoples are living side by side in the same communities. This calls for even more participation skills to make sure that all of the cultural perspectives have a voice in the work of the school.

> The vitality of a culture and a country is enhanced by redefining and rediscovering its cultural self. This vitality comes about only through the process of understanding, appreciating, and incorporating the diverse cultural traditions of its people (Astuto et al., 1994, p. 91).

Participation needs to lead to products or decisions or common directions. It is crucial for a group that has participated well to see the fruits of their labors actualized. For the administration to ignore totally the thinking of a group will result in little motivation to participate in the future. This is why the administration meets regularly with teams or team leaders, keeps abreast of all that is going on, and encourages the ideas and implementation efforts of the teams. In addition, it is crucial for the administration to share all the necessary data, mandates, guidelines, and parameters ahead of time so that whatever plans are developed can be affirmed by the administration. The following describes efforts of a principal to do just that:

> Crockett developed a process so all teachers and school personnel play a part in the school's leadership. The principal meets often with variously configured groups and relies on teachers'

recommendations to make decisions regarding practice. As they reflect, make decisions, consider challenges, and refine practice gain, teachers own the decision. This way, the school avoids the 'us against them' split between administrative and teaching staff. (Gideon & Erlandson, 2001, p. 16)

Guarding one's use of language is another important aspect. "Language has the potential of inviting or closing off participation. Particular words and phrases can actually enhance the atmosphere of participation" (Williams, 1993, p. 75). Unknowingly, one may cut off participation by the very language one employs. "Some teachers and I came up with this plan; do you all agree it is pretty good?" There is not much leeway for disagreement or even improvement of the plan in that comment. "I really liked that team's presentation. What do you think?" Again, it would appear unwise to contradict the presentation after a comment like that. "Wherever did that idea come from?" or "That's the craziest thing I've ever heard." These responses really stop participation in its tracks, especially if the one leading the group is an administrator.

The following are some alternative ways of expressing the above. "Some teachers and I worked on this plan. What do you notice about it? What are things you like about it? How might we add to this plan or change it to improve it?" Next, "let's thank this team for their presentation. Now, what do you remember particularly from it? How could this presentation be improved? Or, what might this team keep in mind as they continue to work on this project?" Occasionally, someone makes a comment that does seem totally off the wall. In those instances, the facilitator might ask, "Tell me, what values are behind your comment?" Or, "Say a little more about that idea." In some cases, what at first seems like an idea out of left field may actually provide a perspective hitherto not thought about. Furthermore, in other cases, it may be possible to affirm the value behind the comment even though its concretion might be unworkable. "Language is powerful. It is also second nature to us. It is easy to be unaware of what our language does to the people around us" (Williams, 1993, p. 75).

Finally, it is important to guard against using too many phrases like, "That's good" or "I like that" or "Excellent idea." These comments sound like positive affirmation. In reality, they embody judgment. It is far better to say a simple, "Thank you for that." That conveys positive regard for the participation but no judgment as to the value of that comment. In this way, the encouragement of participation has been accomplished without the group sensing the leader has judged some comments as worthy and other comments as unworthy.

■ ACTIVITY ONE—ENSURE PARTICIPATIVE PLANNING

Description

Two practical suggestions can go a long way to ensure effective participative planning. The first sounds simple, but it is crucial: Spend time formulating the specific question that the planning is to answer. This can be done by the whole group or by a small group ahead of time with opportunity for input or polishing by the whole group. A group can begin with the phrase "How can we?"

The question can either be a very specific focused question or a somewhat general focused question. A specific one might be: "How can we more successfully mainstream all of our special needs students into our regular classrooms?" Or "How can we prepare the entire school community for the schedule changes we are about to initiate?" A more general one might be: "How can we foster more student-centered classrooms?" or "How can we prepare our staff to instruct in ways that speak to many different learning styles?" The gift of questions like these is that they narrow the field; they provide the parameters that help to focus thinking.

The second suggestion when planning is to follow a process: Begin with individual thinking, followed by team brainstorming, and ending with whole-group discussion. It is crucial to allow time for individual thinking. Simplistically, there are two kinds of thinkers. The first are quick thinkers. These are the people that raise their hands with a response before one has even finished the question. The second are careful thinkers. These are people that appreciate looking at several angles before coming up with a clear thought. It is important to capitalize on both kinds of thinkers.

Team brainstorming allows everyone to share their thinking in a relatively nonthreatening environment of two or three colleagues. This step allows thinking to be challenged and clarified. Sometimes the thinking of one is combined with the thinking of another to come up with a more complete or more solid response. It is helpful to follow this step of team brainstorming even if there are only four people around the table. Four people offer three different pairing possibilities.

The final step is whole-group discussion. Teams get to share their brainstorming with the whole group and discern what the whole group is indicating as the answer to the original question.

Methodology

1. Decide the general arena of what the planning needs to be. The whole group can do this or a small group ahead of time can suggest the arena of planning to the whole group.

2. If the whole group is doing this, have each individual write his or her own question (e.g., "How can we . . . ?").

3. Then have each team hear what its team members have created.

4. Suggest that each team build one question out of all the team member's contributions.

5. Have each team share its one question.

6. Build one question for the whole group out of these team questions.

Note that this flow has honored the three steps of individual thinking, team brainstorming, and whole-group discussion. This is a valuable format for any planning that makes sure everyone has input into the process.

Example

Four teams offered the following four questions on the issue or concern of preparing the school community for a school schedule change to year-round schooling.

1. How can we respond to the objections people will have?

2. How can we enlist many constituencies to help us in the planning process?

3. How can we communicate this direction in a way that will make sense to our school constituencies?

4. How can we demonstrate the values of different schedules and why we are suggesting the year-round schedule?

Using these four questions, the final single question might look like: How can we enlist many school constituencies to research the best school schedule and help us communicate the results to the public?

Metacognitive Insights

The structure of individual thinking, team brainstorming, and whole-group discussion is extremely helpful in dealing with the nay-sayers and the contentious staff members. They are allowed to speak their piece within their teams, but the whole team has the final say. This allows the whole-group discussion to be much more productive and positive.

■ ACTIVITY TWO—EMPOWER IMPLEMENTATION TEAMS

Description

In the last two or three decades, it has been very common for school administrations to create advisory teams around various concerns or topics. What they actually need are implementation teams. Implementation teams are part of the entire planning process; when the planning is completed, each team takes responsibility for implementing its segment of the plan. Administrators need help and support. Teachers need to experience the bigger picture beyond the classroom.

Methodology

1. The planning process needs to move toward establishing three to five broad strategies to accomplish the stated vision and goals.

2. At that point strategy implementation teams need to be established. Eliciting volunteers or making assignments can accomplish this.

3. When the teams are defining their desired accomplishments for upcoming quarters, they need to be realistic. They are the ones who

will be carrying them out, and they are already busy. They need to choose accomplishments that are both realistic and motivating.

4. Then, looking at the desired accomplishments of the first quarter, they need to figure out what steps are needed, who will do them, and by when they need to be done.

5. It is crucial for the administration to support the work of the implementation teams. Concerns or parameters need to be communicated before the teams meet to avoid having an administrator indicate that such and such cannot happen because. . . .

Example

The example (Table 1.1) shows a year's plan for accomplishments. The group was composed of school staff and representatives from the business community. They made a plan for the next year of their business-education partnership work. This was their second Partnership Conference.

Down the side of the table are the four broad strategies this group came up with. Across the top are the four quarters with the months designated. The four strategy teams created the desired accomplishments for their particular strategy. They targeted two accomplishments per strategy per quarter. Once their projections were completed, they shared these with the whole group for a whole-group consensus. This allowed the group to pose questions of clarity as well as offer additional information for them to consider as they proceeded toward implementation.

The strategy teams returned to focus on just the first quarter. They worked on the individual steps to bring about the accomplishments they had targeted. Once the steps were clear, they then designated who would accomplish each step and by when each step would be accomplished. This is documented in Table 1.2.

Note that Template 1 is a blank to be used in planning a year's accomplishments through several strategies by four quarters.

Template 2 is a blank to be used in the detailed action planning for a specific accomplishment. There are columns for what the action step is, who will do it, and by when it will be accomplished.

Metacognitive Insights

While there may be a few things in a school administrator's tasks that only an administrator should handle, a majority of tasks can be sent to the implementation teams. Other than dialing 911 in an emergency, an administrator needs to think twice about handling a task, always asking first which one of the implementation teams the task can be directed to.

ACTIVITY THREE—ENCOURAGE PEER COACHING

Description

The research on peer coaching suggests that this is the decisive step in guaranteeing that new instructional strategies and techniques get transferred into the classroom regularly. When peer coaching is initiated with thought

Table 1.1   School Business Partnership Planned Accomplishments by School Quarters

Quarter / Strategy	MAR APR MAY	JUN JUL AUG	SEP OCT NOV	DEC JAN FEB
Establishing physical presence	Send letters to business leaders.	Create staff job descriptions.	Hold a fundraiser.	Distribute a report to community.
	Distribute school business partnership logo.	Develop slide show.	Initiate a business-education week.	Establish staff location.
Answering the questions of what business we are in	Form a marketing committee.	Identify funding resources.	Hold a school staff awareness event.	Produce a video.
	Develop budgetary process.	Review past survey results.	Carry out a media blitz.	Implement a speakers bureau.
Creating operational strategies	Set up a stakeholder steering committee.	Hold a business-education conference.	Include industry in curriculum rewrites.	Create incentive programs.
	Negotiate released time for participation.	Have teachers shadow business.	Have students and parents shadow business.	Have classroom presentations by employees.
Identifying the resources	Inventory current resources.	Distribute a resource handbook.	Hold career expo.	Implement a regional product fair.
	Create a designated central clearing house.	Distribute industry videos.	Establish student apprentice program.	Create a career resource center in secondary schools.

Table 1.2 Implementation Steps

Accomplishment	What	Who	When
Designate a central clearinghouse	Staff person search (contact retirees)	Ken	April
	Staff search (parent volunteers)	Lee	April during citywide PTA meetings
	Space search	Paul	May
	Determine equipment needs	Dick	April
	Follow-up meeting May 28, 4:00 PM	Chris	By May 15

beforehand and is carried out well, it is a nonthreatening way of helping teachers bring new strategies and techniques into their teaching. Often peer coaching is introduced as a follow-up to a specific series of workshops or inservice activities. This way the staff has a common training experience with common language and thus common skills to transfer to the classroom.

Much has been written on peer coaching. The examples here focus on just a few tools to enable peer coaching to happen.

Methodology

Gottesman suggests five steps to incorporate into a peer coaching flow (Gottesman, 2000, p. 33):

1. Request for a peer visit

2. Peer visit

3. Review of notes and consideration of possibilities

4. Conversation after the visit

5. Reflection on the whole process

The request for a peer visit includes asking for a visit, setting up a time for meeting, and then preparing for the visit itself. The peer visit involves the peer spending 15 minutes to an hour in the class observing the specific item that has been requested to be observed. Having taken some kind of notes during the visit, the peer who has visited then reviews those notes and considers what might be three recommendations to offer the peer about the item observed. During the conversation after the visit, the peer who has visited sticks to the focus and uses questions more than personal reflections to engage the peer who has been visited in a process of thinking through the visit and its ramifications. Finally the peer who has visited initiates some questions to help the one who has been visited reflect on the whole coaching process.

Gottesman also distinguishes among three kinds of peer involvement (Gottesman, 2000, p. 31). The first she calls Peer Watching. This involves a peer just sitting in the classroom observing. No follow-up visit is required because all the peer has done is just being present in the classroom. The second she calls Peer Feedback. During the conversation before the visit, the requesting teacher outlines precisely what the observing peer is to watch for. That peer takes notes only on that specific item. Then during the conversation after the visit, the peer turns over the notes from that observation and initiates reflection on that observation. The third she calls Peer Coaching. This time, in addition to specific notes on the item to be observed, the peer observing can add additional suggestions and recommendations. It is suggested, however, that the peer who has observed keeps the recommendations to no more than three so as not to overwhelm the teacher who has requested the observation.

Example

Items the Teacher Might Ask a Peer to Observe

1. Wait time
2. Equity in calling on both male and female students
3. Context and instruction for an activity
4. Explaining and assigning cooperative roles
5. The use of higher-order questions
6. Monitoring cooperative groups
7. Chunking out a lecture

Guidelines for the Previsit Conversation

1. Identify the focus.
2. Create the observation tool.
3. Settle on the time for the visit.
4. Discuss where to sit.
5. Review specific class data and lesson plan.
6. Decide on the postvisit conversation time.

Guidelines for the Postvisit Conversation

1. Offer thanks for the chance to visit.
2. Share the data observed.
3. Process the data.
4. Turn over the notes.
5. Offer no more than three recommendations (in the third kind of involvement, called Peer Coaching).
6. Reflect on the coaching process.

Table 1.3 offers an example of a form filled out by the observer.

Table 1.3   Peer Observation Form

OBSERVEE:	Marion Jackson	DATE: Oct. 14
SCHOOL:	Boone Elementary School	
LESSON FOCUS:	Change of seasons	
FOCUS OF OBSERVATION:	Instruction for a cooperative group activity	
OBSERVER:	Joshua Miller	
FEEDBACK:	These are the instructions Ms. Jackson gave: "Get into your cooperative groups. If you were the organizer last time, this time you will be the encourager. If you were the encourager last time, this time you will be the recorder. If you were the recorder last time, this time you will be the organizer. Read the paragraph individually. Then discuss the paragraph and find three insights about your season. Draw a picture and write the insights at the bottom of the page."	
COMMENTS FROM OBSERVEE:	"The instructions I gave were okay. What I forgot to say was how much time I would give them to do this. Also I didn't say anything about where the materials were. Consequently, I had a lot of group questions about specifically what materials we were to use. Also, many groups were not anywhere near finished when I had planned for them to be finished because I neglected to give them a time frame."	
PROPOSED STRATEGIES FOR FUTURE LESSONS:	"I will jot down in my planning book these parts of cooperative group instructions: roles, clear definition of the task, time frame, and the specific materials. That will help me remember what to write out ahead of time for the instructions."	

Templates 3 and 4 offer blank forms that can be used when initiating peer coaching.

Metacognitive Insights

It is important to make clear to participants that peer coaching is totally different from administrative evaluations. The experience of the pair of teachers is totally confidential. In addition, control always rests in the hands of the teacher requesting the peer's visit. That teacher is the one who suggests what will be observed. The observing teacher only offers data relative to the skill being observed. Gradually more trust may develop and the teacher being observed might be willing for other comments. At the beginning, however, it is important to stick to only the skill being observed.

Unlike mentors, each of the peers relates to the other on an equal basis. Each of the pairs will be an observer and will be observed.

Finally, it is important to understand that the whole role of the observer coach is to encourage the thinking processes of the one being observed. Consequently, the greatest skill needed by the "coach" is the ability to ask open-ended and thought-provoking questions.

ACTIVITY FOUR—ESTABLISH A MENTORING PROGRAM

Description

Two factors in schools today emphasize the need for a well-structured mentoring program. The first factor is the imminent retiring of huge numbers of experienced teachers, and the second is the large dropout rate of new teachers. "In the first decade of the 21st century, schools will need approximately 2.5 million new teachers" (Salzman, 2002, p. 1). Many teachers are retiring, leaving a huge gap in the teaching force. Many of these teachers are some of the best, most-qualified teachers in the schools. Somehow, their wisdom needs to be passed on to new teachers.

Furthermore, many teachers do not make it past the first three years or so after they begin to teach (Salzman, 2001, p. 1). The job can seem daunting and overwhelming. An experienced teacher can share some of the practical tools he or she has developed to deal with some of the issues a new teacher faces, which is one valuable outcome of a mentoring program that matches up experienced teachers with newer teachers in a supportive and instructive relationship. This contrasts with the peer coaching model that pairs teachers up on a more or less equal plane. In mentoring, it is clear from the start which one is more experienced and which one is being mentored.

Two sources outline remarkably similar criteria for teaching competencies on which the mentor can focus. Salzman (2001) calls these "Criteria of competent teaching" (p. 24). One source comes from the Pathwise Performance Assessment from the Educational Testing Service (ETS) (Salzman, 2001, pp. 23–24). Another source comes from Charlotte Danielson's book *Enhancing Professional Practice: A Framework for Teaching.* Table 1.4 provides the high-level headings used by both Pathwise and Danielson.

Table 1.4   Comparison of Teacher Mentoring Criteria

Pathways Performance Assessment	Danielson's Framework for Teaching
1. Planning	1. Planning
2. Learning environment	2. Classroom environment
3. Teaching	3. Instruction
4. Professionalism	4. Professionalism

SOURCES: Adapted from Salzman, J. (2002). *The promise of mentoring* (p. 24). Chicago: Robin Fogarty & Associates; and Pitton, D. E. (2000). *Mentoring novice teachers* (pp. 72–78). Arlington Heights, IL: SkyLight Professional Development.

Each set of headings in the table has a lot of detail under each category. But perhaps it is better to let the mentor fill in the details with what is most crucial for the mentor of what the mentor observes is most needed by the mentee.

Skills needed by the mentor are very similar to skills needed by any coach. Salzman (2001, p. 30) offers four major skills:

1. The ability to build trust and rapport with the mentee

2. The art of questioning the mentees to promote their own thinking

3. The skill of responding to the mentee in nonjudgmental ways

4. The goal of empowering mentees to be autonomous and self-directed

This calls for a very different approach with the mentee from that used to teach in the classroom. It is tempting in the classroom to assume that as the teacher one has the right answers and needs to impart these to the students. (Today, however, even in the classroom, many teachers are moving toward facilitating students finding the answers themselves rather than giving them the answers.) When working with the mentee, it is even more imperative that the mentor ask questions that will spark the mentee's own thinking. Needless to say it is much more helpful to convey to mentees that the mentees have good answers inside them. This is why it is suggested that the mentor always respond in nonjudgmental ways so that the mentee can gain more and more self-confidence. In other words, the mentor's overall goal is to work out of the job of being the mentor!

Keeping that in mind, notice how the following questions from Pitton (2000, pp. 49–50) help to foster the mentee's own thinking:

1. How do you feel about your lesson today?

2. How did you think it went?

3. How much of what you intended got accomplished today?

4. What in today's lesson would you like to talk about?

5. Why do you think that student did that?

6. What clues in the student's behavior led you to think this?

7. What might be another way to handle that?

8. What might be the result if you did _____?

9. How might (mentee's action) impact (student's behavior or response)?

The nature of the mentor-mentee relationship is different from the peer-to-peer relationship in peer coaching. In the mentor-mentee relationship structure, as mentioned before, it is clear that the mentor has more teaching experience. It is assumed more easily that the mentor will have suggestions. However, it is still crucial that the mentor guide the relationship, build trust, empower the mentee, and learn to respond in nonjudgmental ways. When done well, a mentor program can be the source of great teacher improvement and great energy for the teaching task. "A well-designed mentoring program breaks through the classroom isolation that stifles many teachers' awareness of potentially better ways of teaching and helping students to achieve their potential. These programs also provide mentors with new ways of energizing themselves" (Salzman, 2001, p. 41).

Methodology

1. Begin with the preobservation conversation similar to the conversation used with peer coaching.

2. Following the actual observation visit in the classroom, hold a postobservation conversation.

3. As with the third kind of involvement in peer coaching, keep concrete suggestions to three. Otherwise, the mentee will become overwhelmed.

4. Mentors might find Template 5 helpful for guiding their journey through the preobservation, observation, and postobservation steps.

5. Mentors might find helpful a simple observation form in Template 6, adapted from Pitton (2001, p. 105).

Example

Tables 1.5 and 1.6 are examples of two kinds of forms to use for writing observation notes.

Metacognitive Insights

If a collegial, nonjudgmental relationship is established, this strategy can do a great deal to boost the morale and confidence of both the mentor and the mentee. The mentee grows with both the practical guidance and the support for the mentee's early teaching. The mentor grows in developing the mentor's skills and in having years of experience acknowledged in a very powerful, structured format.

Table 1.5   Mentor Visit Form

Preobservation Visit	
Focus	Gender equity in students called on
Observation tools	Seating chart—check mark next to each person called on
Logistics: Time, where to sit	Wednesday, third period; chair in back of room
Class data	All test in top 20% in standardized tests; ethnically mixed
Lesson plan	10-minute video on ecological issues, partner sharing, questioning of individuals
Postobservation visit time	Thursday, fourth period
Observation Notes	
The teacher set up the video by asking half of the class to look at the details of the situation described. Then she asked the other half of the class to concentrate on suggestions for correcting the situation. The students paid close attention to the video. A couple of pairs did not stay on task but focused during the questioning time. She called on two of the male students and eight of the female students.	
Postobservation Visit	
Offer thanks	Thank you for letting me observe that lesson.
Data sharing	Here is the class seating chart with the check marks beside those you called on.
Data processing	What did you notice? *I called on far more female students than male students. I was so conscious of making it more equal, I had no idea I had done so poorly.*
Questioning	What might be some of the reasons for that? *Well, the female students I called on are always so eager to respond. Usually they are so on target with their answers, I guess I don't like to risk a student giving me the wrong answer.*
Recommendations	Maybe you could plan ahead of time who to call on. Also, you might alert them that you are going to alternate male and female students to call on.
Reflections on mentor process	What is working for you in our mentoring process? *At first I was extremely nervous with you being in the classroom. Now I actually look forward to your visits. I really want to become a good teacher.* How might we improve our process together? *I would like to visit your class sometime and just see you teach for a while.*
Next observation focus	What could we work on next? *I am concerned about how I give instructions for group task. I would like you to script what I say. (etc.)*

Table 1.6   Observation Notes

Mentor: <u>Ms. Jackson</u>	Date: <u>Feb 3, 2005</u>
Mentee: <u>Mr. Owens</u>	Class/Grade: <u>7th</u>

I saw . . .	The students were amazingly focused and most stayed on task.
	I noticed that all paired teams but one used good attentive listening skills when their partners were talking.
	One pair was distracted, but Mr. Owens noticed that and moved closer to them and they got on task.
I heard . . .	Students freely asked a couple of questions to clarify the directions.
	Mr. Owens then asked again if everyone understood the directions.
	I walked around and heard excellent discussions about the material.
	Only one pair had difficulty filling out the graphic organizer.
I thought . . .	Mr. Owens has really created great rapport with his students.
	The questions the students asked for clarification of the directions were thoughtful questions.
	I'd like to see Mr. Owens move around more and listen more attentively to the pair conversations going on.

2

Illuminating Visible Achievements

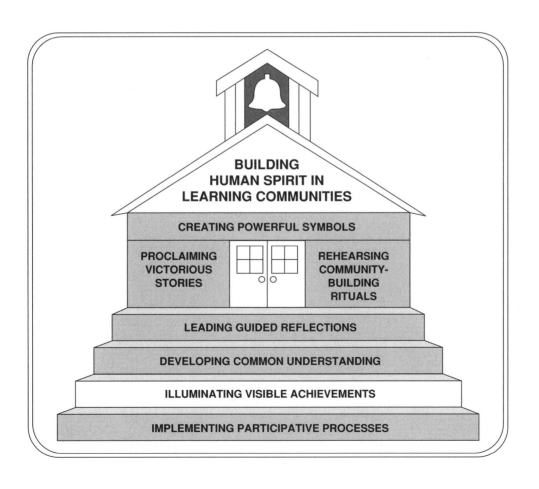

BUILDING
HUMAN SPIRIT IN
LEARNING COMMUNITIES

CREATING POWERFUL SYMBOLS

PROCLAIMING VICTORIOUS STORIES

REHEARSING COMMUNITY-BUILDING RITUALS

LEADING GUIDED REFLECTIONS

DEVELOPING COMMON UNDERSTANDING

ILLUMINATING VISIBLE ACHIEVEMENTS

IMPLEMENTING PARTICIPATIVE PROCESSES

The environment remains uncreated until we interact with it; there is no describing it until we engage with it. Abstract planning divorced from action becomes a cerebral activity of conjuring up a world that does not exist.

—Margaret J. Wheatley, 1992,
Leadership and the New Science (p. 37)

A school decided that its emphasis for an entire year would be adding student portfolios to the repertoire of evidence of student learning. This process began with teacher training workshops to familiarize the teachers with the process of initiating student portfolios. They decided that the visible achievement for this process would be a Portfolio Night during which the students would share their portfolios with their parents or guardians. The teachers planned this three or four months ahead of time so the event would be very special. The hallways were spectacularly decorated with student work. Refreshments were served to parents once they finished seeing their child's portfolio. The teachers trained their students in how to lead the parents through the sharing of their portfolios. Invitations, which were handwritten by all the students, went home to the parents and guardians. The teachers were overwhelmed when they tallied up that 95 percent of the students had an adult present that night. This was a stellar happening that involved the administration, the teachers, the students, and the parents in a project that dramatically enhanced student learning.

Human beings need constant unarguable reminders that progress is being made. Without such incontrovertible reminders, it is easy to slip into burnout or cynicism. Hence there is a crucial need for what I am calling visible achievements. These visible achievements are vital for fostering spirit.

■ CLARITY ON VISIBLE ACHIEVEMENTS

There have been schools and districts that have spent three or four years doing research, collecting data, conducting surveys, and creating a vision. At that point many wonder why people aren't excited any more. Research, data collection, surveys, and visioning all need to proceed continuously. However, if something visible is not accomplished relatively soon, disbelief grows, cynicism increases, and burnout deepens. This is why the concept of visible achievements is so vital. In three to six months, one or more visible achievements can occur. Perhaps in the planning process, a huge goal has been outlined. This concept of the visible achievement raises the possibility that a small chunk of that larger goal can be made visible in a short amount of time. First, a visible achievement is, obviously, visible. Especially at the beginning of a process, achievements need to be seen easily and noted by as many people as possible. Second, a visible achievement is something that can be accomplished, displayed, or up and running in three to six months. Third, a visible achievement is specific enough that it can be accomplished in that short a time. Finally, the process of carrying out a specific, visible achievement provides information on how to keep implementing other parts of a plan or how to complete the remainder of a plan. "The environment remains uncreated until we interact with it; there is no describing it until we engage with it. Abstract planning divorced from action becomes a cerebral activity of conjuring up a world that does not exist" (Wheatley, 1992, p. 37).

Very often people come up with grand goals such as: All students will be at reading level in three years. That is all well and good, but what are the concrete vehicles that will allow that to happen? Perhaps they are vehicles such as cross–grade-level reading events, an afterschool tutoring program, a reading incentive system, and so forth.

A visible achievement is something that is planned for, worked on, and finally accomplished and over. Many people are willing to put their energies behind a defined, finite project as opposed to a committee that goes on for years and years.

FOCUS ON DEEP, UNDERLYING ISSUES   ■

When determining what visible achievements to carry out, it is crucial to target a visible achievement that deals with a significant depth issue. It does not need to be a complex achievement to address a deep, underlying concern. Senge (1990) has taught us a great deal about systems thinking. One crucial insight is to avoid making individuals or events the issue or cause of difficulties.

> The systems perspective tells us that we must look beyond individual mistakes or bad luck to understand important problems. We must look beyond personalities and events. We must look into the underlying structures which shape individual actions and create the conditions where types of events become likely. (Senge, 1990, pp. 42–43)

In other words, Senge pushes us to look at the structures that give rise to the issue we are concerned with. A shift in the structure not only can create different individual behaviors but also can create an environment that will foster the implementation of visible achievements. In addition, the more the visible achievements can address unhelpful structures the longer the impact of the achievements will be.

Thinking this way at first may seem depressing. The thought of moving on an unhelpful structure can seem very daunting. "But it is very important to understand that when we use the term 'systemic structure' we do not just mean structure outside the individual. The nature of structure in human systems is subtle because we are part of the structure" (Senge, p. 44). Standing within unhelpful structures can bestow upon us a unique insight as to what can realistically be done to make a shift. The good news is that those who are within a structure have the possibility of knowing how to go about transforming it.

> The reason that structural explanations are so important is that only they address the underlying causes of behavior at a level that patterns of behavior can be changed. Structure produces behavior,

and changing underlying structures can produce different patterns of behavior. (Senge, 1990, p. 53)

When analysis of the structures is done well, key leverage points for change can be discerned. When this happens, it becomes apparent that even small, targeted actions can make a huge difference (Senge, 1990, p. 64). Picking up on our previous section on participative processes, obviously the more people, the more perspectives involved in this process of analysis, the greater the possibility of finding leverage points that can have powerful impacts.

■ THE EMPHASIS ON STANDARDS AND TESTING

Because the concern of this book is building spirit in learning communities, it is necessary to call attention to the huge emphasis on standards and testing today. While appropriate forms of accountability are helpful in the educational process, there is a point where an overemphasis on standards and testing can be harmful to spirit. "An education reform movement rooted in standards, testing, and selectivity is a movement that embraces competition as the driving force behind institutional productivity... School survival will be decided by consumers in a high-stakes games for schools, teachers, and students" (Astuto, Clark, Read, McGree, & Fernandez, 1994, p. 13). The heavy emphasis on standards and testing creates environments of competition and individualism. Therefore, it is crucial that the visible achievements chosen do not feed into or enhance destructive competition. (Note that some forms of competition are very helpful.) In addition, the tight top-down control as seen in some state accountability systems can convey a lack of trust in local educators' competencies to carry out their jobs (Astuto et al., 1994, p. 51). All of these can be extremely deleterious to fostering spirit.

> There is an alternative view of education that sees schools as communities of learners, young and old, committed to supporting one another in the quest to fulfill their human potential. The accumulated evidence on successful schools and student achievement strongly suggests that competitive environments shatter the conditions of trust, caring, and cooperation that are most conducive to learning, innovation, and creativity and that those environments have the most negative consequences for those learners least able to compete successfully. Positive reinforcement and attainable challenges, requisites for learning, are nearly impossible to sustain in an environment of winners and losers. (Astuto et al., 1994, p. 14)

When a school or school team chooses a visible achievement, achievements that foster conditions of trust, caring, and cooperation are high priorities. Likewise, environments of trust, caring, and cooperation are the best environments for enabling the successful completion of visible achievements. One can readily see that without thought and care, the high emphasis on standards and testing can lead to environments of competition, distrust, and despair.

THE PRIMARY FOCUS OF STUDENT LEARNING AND ACHIEVEMENT ■

In the midst of a scramble for resources today, in the midst of a variety of needs within a school, the laser-sharp focus needs to be on student learning and achievement.

> The centrality of student learning is the driving purpose of all activities. . . . Major school improvement efforts can be sustained only when the context promises student learning. Otherwise, the changes in organizational behavior and the struggle for implementation are likely to be perceived as too stressful to be worthwhile. Essentially, the mission is lost unless learning remains at the core. (Joyce, Wolf, & Calhoun, 1993, pp. 19–20)

The visible achievements that are created and implemented need to contribute to this focus on student learning and student achievement. Only those visible achievements are worthy of the extra time and effort it will take to pull them off. Only those achievements will speak to the deep commitment the teachers have for educating their students.

A high school located in a very poverty-stricken area of a large urban center in California had a high population of students whose native language was not English. Many of these students were still in the process of learning English and fitting into a new high school situation. The science teacher decided to challenge them to create a robot that would be entered into a national robot contest. The students surprised the teacher by engaging themselves completely in this project. To complete the project, they had to learn a great deal of math and a lot about science. Everyone was delighted when their robot won regionally, allowing the team to join the national competition. Imagine the excitement when this high school group not only won the top prize nationally but even beat the team from a major university. This visible achievement changed the lives of those students. It also challenged the notion that students in such a high school could not really perform well.

SIGN OF COMMITMENT ■

"How do you know people are committed? Because they are taking action" (Jaworski, 1996, p. 133). Visible achievements become a sign of commitment. They become a sign of belief that it is possible to create effective change. Visible achievements become a sign of the belief that learning can occur even in unlikely places, even with students from difficult situations. Because visible achievements spark belief and faith, they have the power to increase the numbers of those willing to work on future visible achievements. "Individual improvement flows from success and increased personal capacity. . . . Success feeds success." (Astuto et al., 1994, p. 46)

The demonstrated commitment and the evidence of great success become tremendous antidotes for the cynicism and burnout that often plagues our schools. One by one the doubters will change their hearts or move out. So much of the work of building spirit is transforming the despair and the cynicism that have grown in our teachers and in our students. "Dramatic successes encourage more and more energy for the task" (Williams, 1997, p. xiv).

■ COMMUNICATING VISIBLE ACHIEVEMENTS

The power of visible achievements is expanded when these achievements are talked about. Many successes going on in schools today remain within the four walls of school. So one of the challenges facing schools today is to find a myriad of ways to proclaim the victories, to broadcast successes way beyond the four walls. Newspapers, radio, television, cable, the Internet, and school newsletters can all become vehicles for getting this good news out.

A related challenge is to ensure that the greater percentage of all communication that goes on is focused on the visible achievements.

> Successful communication focuses on visible achievements—those events and processes that directly and concretely express the positive changes in the local educational system. When communicated clearly, participants can see exactly what change took place, how it was implemented, and why it worked. (Williams, 1997, p. xiv)

This is not easy. The greater percentage of a faculty meeting needs to be focused on visible achievements. The greater percentage of faculty lounge conversation needs to center on small or large visible achievements. The greater percentage of a department meeting needs to zero in on visible achievements and what is working in the classroom. Conversations need to examine exactly what made things work or how to improve what happened. It is one huge task to pull off visible achievements. It is another huge task to spread the word about these great achievements.

■ ACTIVITY FIVE—GENERATE A COMMON PRACTICAL VISION

Description

Two practical tools to help spread a common practical vision are a Hopes and Expectations conversation and a Practical Vision cardstorming workshop.

The Hopes and Expectations conversation is a gentle and informal way to get a group to articulate what kinds of overt and latent visions they have for the school. The Practical Vision cardstorming workshop helps a group in a more formal way to crystallize its vision.

Methodology for Hopes and Expectations Conversation

(Refer to Chapter 4 for information on leading focused conversations.) The following questions might be used in a Hopes and Expectations conversation:

1. What are some of this school's accomplishments in the last year or so?

2. What are some of your own work accomplishments in the last year or so that you are especially proud of?

3. What are some of your hopes for this school three to five years from now?

4. What are some of the accomplishments you look for in the next three to five years?

5. What are some of the common themes in our responses?

6. For even some of these hopes to happen, what are some of the concrete implications for this school, for our staff?

Methodology for a Practical Vision Cardstorming Workshop

A Practical Vision cardstorming workshop might consist of the following:

1. Mention that the process to be used will involve individual, team, and whole-group thinking.

2. Have the group look at the workshop focus question and polish it if necessary. (A question might be: What will we see and hear going on in three years in this school that indicates we are enabling all of our students to grow academically, socially, physically, and emotionally?)

3. Suggest that individuals think about five to seven possible responses to the question.

4. Have small teams of three to five people share some of their responses with each other.

5. Have the small teams choose five to seven of their team's best responses and write them on 5 × 8 cards, one item per card, using magic markers and writing in large letters.

6. Prepare 9 or 10 cards with different symbols on them to put up in a row in the front of the room. Also prepare tape loops or some other method for affixing the cards to the front wall.

7. Once the teams have completed their card writing, have each team pass up one or two of their clearest cards. (Assure them that eventually all the cards will come up.)

8. Read each card out loud and put up the card at random after you have read the card. When several are up, ask the group where they see connections or relationships.

9. Ask for another round of cards—perhaps ones that are different from the ones already up.

10. Again, ask for connections or relationships. When you have five or six clusters forming, put up initial one- or two-word holding titles on 3 × 5 sticky notes.

11. Have the group put symbols on cards that naturally gravitate toward a cluster or card that is on the front wall. Have them pass up all the cards whether they have symbols on them or not.

12. Put up these remaining cards, starting first with the ones without symbols to get the spread of data as soon as possible.

13. Be sure to read all of the cards out loud as you put them up.

14. For each column cluster, ask if the holding title still stands.

15. Then ask for one or two more words, perhaps adjectives, to clarify and pinpoint what the column is talking about.

16. Write that title on a bordered card and put on the top of the column.

17. If a column only has one card, either add more cards to flesh out the column or see if that one card now fits in one of the other columns.

18. Ask some kind of reflective question to close:
    a. Which column interests you the most?
    b. Which column will be hardest to realize? Which column will be easiest to realize?

19. Thank the group for their hard work.

Example

A high school was concerned about its at-risk students. The workshop produced the Practical Vision chart shown in Table 2.1.

A chart blank for cardstorming can be found in Template 7.

Metacognitive Insights

The more that pieces of the Practical Vision can come directly from staff participants rather than imposed on them from the administration, the more ownership and buy-in from the staff there will be. Needless to say, the more staff ownership and buy-in that can be generated, the more energy and commitment for the tasks there will be.

■ ACTIVITY SIX—INCULCATE A STRATEGIC PLANNING AND IMPLEMENTATION PROCESS

Description

There are many available processes to use for strategic planning and implementation. Some of the criteria one can use to distinguish among

Table 2.1 Sample Vision

Useful & Sufficient Facilities & Equipment	Comfortable and Challenging Climate	Relevant Progressive Professional Development	Active Student-Centered Learning	Community Partnerships in Learning	Skills to Manage Life	Active Respectful Citizenship
Media-centered school	Umbrella of ethics	Teachers observing teachers	Students are busy	Community guests in classroom	Day care	Course to investigate ethics
Involved computer usage	Comfortable and fun	Sharing sessions on topics & interests	Students are working in small groups	Industry teaching students	Problem solving	Learning social responsibility
New classroom facilities	No jargon	Teachers teaching teachers	Teachers facilitate learning	Support staff teaching	Teaching thinking	Advanced students assisting others
	Relaxed, open meetings	Rotated paid sabbaticals	Students publish writing	Students interviewing adults	Project-based learning	
	Excited learning	Teaching staff to use technology	Students teach peers	Business people in classroom	Real world application	
		Administrators in classrooms	Students attend meetings	Parents in classroom	Life skills	
		Administrators teaching	Students look interested	Students demonstrate skills to parents	Team work	
			Students involved in building operations		Interpersonal skills	

them include: Are they relatively simple? Are they relatively economical time-wise? Do they move a group toward implementable projects and activities? Do they help the group to create implementation teams? Do they leave a group with a realistic, practical timeline for accomplishing the projects and activities? The process outlined in the Methodology section suggests a flow that does all of the above.

Methodology

There are some crucial steps that follow the data-gathering and research phases. As mentioned in Chapter 1, it is certainly helpful for the group to create the one question that they want the planning phase to answer. Following that, it is helpful to create a practical vision followed by some work describing the current and suspected obstacles to reaching the practical vision. Then looking at both the vision and the obstacles the group can create an action framework describing the action arenas necessary for reaching the practical vision and dealing with the obstacles. From this framework, the group can discern three to five broad strategies that encompass all the action arenas. At this point, it is helpful to divide the group into strategy teams. The teams can delineate the first-year accomplishments and the detailed action plan for the first chunk of time—a quarter or a semester. Ongoing *check-signals* meetings are always crucial, as well as new detailed action planning for the next chunk of time. Figure 2.2 illustrates this suggested flow.

The reflective questions in Table 2.2 are helpful for determining what steps are particularly crucial for a particular school or group. Process questions are the ones to ask to help the group brainstorm that phase.

Metacognitive Insights

It is possible to carry out each of the steps presented in Table 2.2 over a two-day period. It is helpful to have someone present who is documenting each step as it is completed. Concluding the workshop by presenting each participant with a document of the plan sends a positive, encouraging message. Continually referring to this document makes it very much a living, dynamic product of the group's hard work.

ACTIVITY SEVEN—CARRY OUT FOCUSED VISIBLE ACCOMPLISHMENTS

Description

First a school determines what its three or four broad strategies will be in the next few years. Then, in looking at the first year, the school can target several visible achievements, which will begin carrying out the broad strategies. It doesn't matter if they are big achievements or small achievements. What matters is that they can be done realistically and that they are visible. Everyone in the school community needs to see things happening.

Figure 2.2   Strategic Planning and Implementation Flow

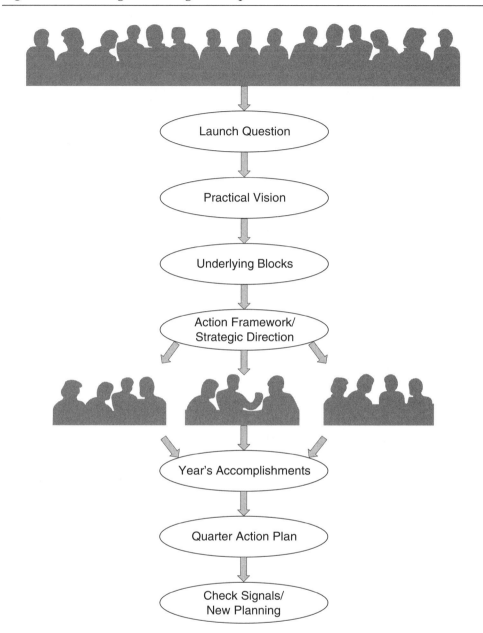

Methodology

1. Determine the broad strategies for the school such as "Creating Learner-Centered Classrooms" or "Establishing Implementation Teams."

2. Lay out the first year of visible achievements. For Creating Learner-Centered Classrooms, there could be two flows: One could be about focused trainings; the second could be about peer coaching. To initiate focused training, the year's flow might look like
   a. First Quarter—Two workshops to train faculty
   b. Second Quarter—Each teacher submits two model lessons

Table 2.2   Reflective and Process Questions for Each Planning Step

Practical vision	**Reflective Questions**
	Is there some indication of a formulated vision or mission statement? What changes do the staff members wish to initiate?
	Process Questions
	What will we see and hear going on in three years that indicates we are accomplishing our mission? What will we hear people saying in three years that indicates we have been successful in carrying out our vision?
Underlying blocks	**Reflective Questions**
	Where does the group seem to be struggling? What overwhelms them? What forms of resistance are in evidence?
	Process Questions
	What are the roadblocks, obstacles, and structures that prevent us from realizing our vision?
Action framework/ Strategic directions	**Reflective Questions**
	What evidence do you discern that indicates the group is ready to move? What tells you that they may not know how to get started?
	Process Questions
	What concrete, realistic, accomplishable actions will bring us closer to the vision and help us overcome our obstacles?
Accomplishment projection	**Reflective Questions**
	Is the group clear about the realistic accomplishments they will perform phased over a set period of time, such as a year?
	Process Questions
	What specific projects or events will bring about our overall goals and objectives? How can we spread those out over a timeline?
Detailed action plan	**Reflective Questions**
	What tells you that the group is paralyzed? What tells you that the tasks are not defined and organized?
	Process questions
	What are the required steps to accomplishing a particular project? Who will be responsible for each step and by when?

    c. Third Quarter—The teachers create a model lesson handbook

    d. Fourth Quarter—The teachers create videotapes of some of the best model lessons

To develop a peer coaching process, the year's flow might look like

    a. First Quarter—Initiate two peer observations a quarter

    b. Second Quarter—Initiate two peer feedback sessions a quarter

    c. Third Quarter—Initiate two full peer coaching sessions a quarter

    d. Fourth Quarter—Change peer coaching partners and do two peer coaching sessions during the quarter

3. Once the year is laid out, the team needs to look at the first quarter and designate the necessary steps to carry out the accomplishments, name people who will be responsible for each step, and plot when each step needs to be done for successful completion. An example of this is given in chart form in Table 2.3.

Table 2.3   Planning Visible Achievements

Creating Learner-Centered Classrooms				
Flow	*First Quarter*	*Second Quarter*	*Third Quarter*	*Fourth Quarter*
1. Initiate focused training	Hold two trainings	Each teacher submits two model lessons	Create model lesson handbook	Videotape model lessons
2. Develop peer-partners, coaching process	Initiate peer observation, 2 per quarter	Initiate peer feedback, 2 per quarter	Initiate peer coaching, 2 per quarter	Change peer coaching 2 per quarter

Regular check-in meetings guarantee smooth implementation.

Template 8 offers a blank form for planning these visible achievements.

Example

A school was concerned that its reading scores were poor. The administration and all of the teachers initiated a daily reading time. In this 20-minute period, everyone, students and teachers, read something personally chosen. This discipline increased the students desire to read, actually getting them excited about reading.

In another example, the leader of a teacher training program that is held over multiple, but not consecutive, days asks each teacher to bring an "artifact," from class that represents something from the training that was implemented in the classroom. Often, even the most skeptical participant can't resist bringing something really great to show. The training leader asks the question, What impact did the artifact have on student learning? Usually, the teacher is amazed and pleased that the strategies implemented worked so well. One example of an artifact might be from Spanish class, where the teacher had groups of students outline one of the group members on chart paper and then write the names of parts of the body in Spanish.

Metacognitive Insights

It is not enough to describe an impressive goal. A school might determine that it needs to increase the number of students meeting or exceeding national standards by 50 percent. That sounds good. However, what is the vehicle the school intends to use to get there? Perhaps it intends to begin an afterschool tutoring program. Launching it might be a first quarter accomplishment. Getting 50 students in it might be a second quarter accomplishment. Expanding to 100 students might be a third quarter accomplishment. Three special coaching classes to prepare these 100 students for an upcoming standardized test might be the fourth quarter accomplishment. A visible achievement is planned for, occurs, and then it is over or has become institutionalized, and the school moves on to the next visible achievement.

ACTIVITY EIGHT—CREATE SCHOOL PORTFOLIOS

Description

School portfolios are very tangible ways of displaying a school's accomplishments. This is a real example of "Seeing is believing." School portfolios are an authentic way of proclaiming the good things happening in a school. A school portfolio is the kind of tool one might show a reporter or a visiting political representative. The contents of a school portfolio can be quite varied. Newspaper articles, pictures, videos, student work, letters from parents or students, teacher anecdotes, charts and tables showing changes over several years—all can be possible portfolio entries.

Methodology

1. Help the group name the three or four major emphases for the year. These could be the strategies developed in the strategic planning process.

2. Invite all the teachers and staff to offer items for the portfolio throughout the school year.

3. Occasionally during staff meetings point out some of the portfolio entries.

4. As the year draws to a close, have teachers or teacher teams choose some of the best items for the final portfolio.

5. Rotate the contents so teacher teams can examine the chosen contributions of other teacher teams and make suggestions.

6. Upon completion of the portfolio, the staff could discuss some of the following questions:
   a. Which items from the portfolio are most noteworthy to you?
   b. Which items pleased you and made you particularly proud?

    c. Which items have surprised you or had you forgotten about?

    d. What is this portfolio telling us about what we have really been able to accomplish this year?

    e. What shifts have you noticed from where we were last year?

    f. Given what is in the portfolio, what might our next steps be?

Example

Table 2.4 shows possible school portfolio contents for an elementary school.

Table 2.4 A School Portfolio

Arena / Grade Level	Accelerating Student Achievement	Deepening Staff Collegiality	Enhancing Parent/Community Connections
K	Pictures of kindergarten orientation event	Vertical team schedule	Parent volunteer weekly schedule
1	Samples of student writing	Common grade-level lessons	Parent career speakers list
2	Student-written books	Video of three team-teaching events	Pictures of students visiting agencies connected to the school
3	Chart showing how all third graders read at or above grade level	Three-month schedule for peer coaching	Pictures of community field trips
4	Student portfolios	Interdisciplinary unit/lesson plans	Videos of student service learning projects

Metacognitive Insights

Imagine what might happen if school portfolios from different years were compared. This would intensify the sense that concrete accomplishments are happening in a school. This has great power in raising the morale of a school's staff. Even the resident cynics have to applaud the evidence in a school portfolio.

ACTIVITY NINE—INITIATE PROFESSIONAL PORTFOLIOS

Description

Many teachers are discovering the power of student portfolios. The very visual, hands-on nature of portfolios clearly demonstrates to students the growth in their skills and learning, thus becoming a crucial motivating factor in their achievement.

> As teachers find success using portfolios with their own students, they realize that portfolios can provide clearer representations of themselves as professionals than the traditional twenty-minute observation by the principal each spring. (Burke, 1997, p. 1)

Consequently, professional portfolios are becoming an additional resource for administrators to gather evidence of the accomplishments of their teachers and for teachers to display to administrators examples of their work that might have gone unnoticed. Some districts are making professional portfolios a mandatory element of the yearly professional review process (Burke, 1997, p. 3).

In addition, many school leaders are discovering that a school leader portfolio is a helpful activity for providing focus to their complex tasks (Dietz, 2001, p. xv). Again, the power of a portfolio is its collection of visible, concrete reminders of notable achievements and victories. Periodically reviewing these can help put momentary setbacks into a broader perspective. The discipline of a portfolio offers an opportunity for personal reflection, out of which can come direction and even new approaches to nagging concerns.

Methodology

1. While there is much complexity to the successful professional portfolio process, I will concentrate on two aspects of the process: the first is a look at the potential items that can go into a professional portfolio; the second is a reflection tool for enabling the collector to decide what to keep in the portfolio.

2. Initially the teacher puts in the portfolio various items that represent what he or she believes are significant signs of his or her teaching expertise. Note that these can be both items that are totally the teacher's creations and items that are samples of student-generated items.

3. After a period of time, it is necessary to review the contents of the portfolio and select items that will be permanent items (i.e., items that will be shown to the administrator).

4. Table 2.5 shows possibilities for teacher-generated portfolio contents, and Table 2.6 shows possibilities for student-generated contents.

5. Table 2.7 is an example of a form to use to help guide the selection process. This form can be attached to each item that the teacher wants to include in the portfolio.

6. The teacher can collect both teacher-generated items and student-generated items to be a part of the professional portfolio.

Table 2.5   Teacher-Generated Portfolio Contents

Record of Resources
<ul><li>Reviews of articles, books, and videotapes</li><li>Summaries of workshops or conferences</li><li>Conversations with specific experts in a field of the teacher's inquiry</li></ul>
Instructional Plans
<ul><li>Unit and lesson plans</li><li>List of lesson/unit opener activities</li><li>Summary of instructional strategy emphases</li><li>Reflective questions</li><li>Compendium of the kind of materials used in instruction</li></ul>
Collegial Observations
<ul><li>Peer observations—of a peer and by a peer</li><li>Mentor observations—of a mentor and by a mentor</li><li>Administrator observations</li><li>Observations by teachers from another school</li></ul>
Media Artifacts
<ul><li>Photographs</li><li>Videos</li><li>Audio tapes</li><li>PowerPoint presentations</li></ul>
Personal Reflections
<ul><li>Unit/lesson reflections</li><li>Daily/weekly journals</li><li>Processing of challenging events</li></ul>
Variety of Assessments
<ul><li>Paper/pencil quizzes/tests</li><li>Observation checklists</li><li>Student interview outline</li><li>Projects assigned</li></ul>

SOURCE: Adapted from Burke, K. (1997). *Designing professional portfolios for change* (p. 54). Arlington Heights, IL: IRI/Skylight.

Table 2.6   Student-Generated Portfolio Contents

Individual Student Work
• Papers • Homework • Graphic organizers • Writings • Presentations • Projects • Art products
Collaborative Student Work
• Pictures of group projects • Presentations on videotape • Debates on audiotape • Experiments
Media Artifacts
• Audiotapes • Videotapes • PowerPoint presentations • Photographs
Student Reflections
• Reflective logs and journals • Reflective pieces in the portfolio • Goal setting and reflections
Evidences of Student Learning
• Tests and quizzes • Standardized test results • Interviews
Parent Responses
• Parent notes or letters • Documentation of phone calls • Summaries of parent visits or conferences • Periodic parent surveys

SOURCE: Adapted from Burke, K. (1997). *Designing professional portfolios for change* (p. 56). Arlington Heights, IL: IRI/Skylight.

Table 2.7   Blank Item Selection Tool for a Portfolio

Item Selection Tool		
Portfolio Focus:		
Personal Professional Development Goal:		
Date	*Item*	*Reason for Inclusion*

SOURCE: Adapted from Burke, K. (1997). *Designing professional portfolios for change* (p. 57). Arlington Heights, IL: IRI/Skylight.

7. The item selection tool shown in Table 2.7 adds a crucial step beyond just collecting material. At some point the teacher needs to review the portfolio contents and select the best items to keep in the portfolio, which are identified by the teacher with the item selection tool. It can be attached to each item selected so that both the teacher and whoever might read it can clearly understand the significance of the item. Template 9 provides this same blank.

Example

Table 2.8 is an example of what an eighth grade science teacher might include in a portfolio concentrating on the unit on energy. Table 2.9 is an example of student-generated items relating to the unit on energy. Table 2.10 is an example of an item selection tool filled out for an item the teacher wants to keep in the portfolio.

Metacognitive Insights

For many people, it is only during times of reflection that connections are made that lead to real learning. The professional portfolio becomes unarguable evidence of what a teacher has accomplished or not accomplished. For the person who tends to forget accomplishments, it provides a memory jogger and thus increases the sense of efficacy. For the person who tends to overstate accomplishments, it provides a reality check and an opportunity to restate goals more realistically. The reflection step helps to clarify the accomplishments in the teacher's mind.

Table 2.8   Teacher-Generated Portfolio Contents for an Eighth Grade Science Teacher

Record of Resources
• Summaries of workshops and speakers at the National Middle School Association Conference • Reviews of two articles on teaching middle school science from Education Leadership • A list of 10 Internet sites helpful for teaching middle school science

Instructional Plans
• Detailed plans for the highly successful unit on energy • Taped video of a 15-minute excerpt of a Discovery Channel presentation raising questions about energy • Samples of case studies used and the initial problems posed in problem-based learning • Reflective questions—Sharing the most surprising pieces of information for you • Predictions of what will happen if the world suddenly runs out of oil • Experiments on energy transference, magazine articles, Internet sites, materials for making models

Collegial Observations
• Peer observation by Mr. Gonzales, a ninth grade science teacher • My observation of Mr. Gonzales's class • Ms. Kang's mentor observation of my class during the energy unit

Media Artifacts
• Photographs of energy experiments • Video of one energy experiment • Audio tapes of two student presentations • Student PowerPoint presentations on energy

Personal Reflections
• My energy unit reflection • Weekly journal during the 3-week energy unit • Reflection about one team that had a hard time working together

Variety of Assessments
• Results of an unannounced quiz • Energy experiment observation checklist • Student self-assessment of the PowerPoint presentation • Graph of the results of the final test

Table 2.9 Student-Generated Portfolio Contents From Eighth Grade Energy Unit

Individual Student Work
• Problem-based learning report from three students • Matrix comparing different kinds of energy from three students • Energy graphic from three students
Collaborative Student Work
• Pictures of group energy experiments • Debate on audiotape of various solutions to the energy crisis
Media Artifacts
• Audiotape of debates • Videotape of energy experiments • PowerPoint presentations of one group's problem-based learning report
Student Reflections
• Reflective logs and journals from three students as they progressed through the energy unit • Reflection from three students on their energy unit goals
Evidences of Student Learning
• Samples of two quizzes and the final test on energy from several students • Interviews with two students who did poorly on the final test
Parent Responses
• Two letters from parents who noted how involved their children were in the energy unit

Table 2.10   Item Selection Tool for Portfolio on Energy Unit

Item Selection Tool		
Portfolio Focus: Eighth-grade unit on energy		
Personal Professional Development Goal: To use a variety of instructional and assessment strategies		
Date	*Item*	*Reason for Inclusion*
January 20	List of 10 Internet sites	These Internet sites opened up my eyes to the resources available on the Internet to help expand my instructional and assessment strategies.
January 25	Detailed unit plan	This is the first time my unit plan has been so detailed and has held such a variety of instructional and assessment strategies.
February 10	Interviews with two students who did poorly on the tests	I was shocked at how much these students had grasped compared to how little they were able to show their knowledge on the final test.

3

Developing Common Understanding

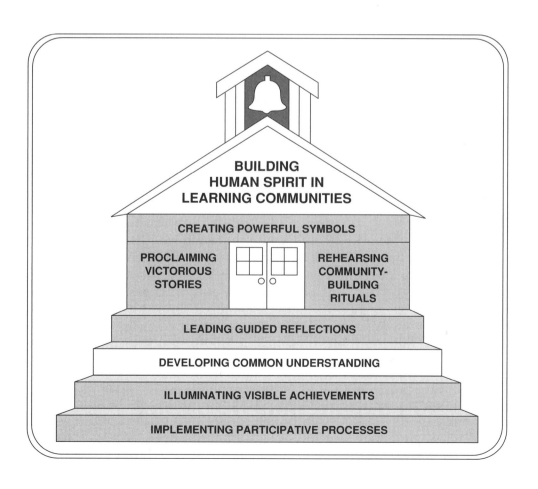

BUILDING
HUMAN SPIRIT IN
LEARNING COMMUNITIES

CREATING POWERFUL SYMBOLS

PROCLAIMING VICTORIOUS STORIES

REHEARSING COMMUNITY-BUILDING RITUALS

LEADING GUIDED REFLECTIONS

DEVELOPING COMMON UNDERSTANDING

ILLUMINATING VISIBLE ACHIEVEMENTS

IMPLEMENTING PARTICIPATIVE PROCESSES

Two overriding conclusions come from this case. One is how central it is for all staff to work on a shared and deeper understanding of a more comprehensive pedagogical philosophy and its relationship to interconnected school structures and associated activities. The second lesson of change is well stated by Prestine: "If anything can be gleaned from this one case, it is that restructuring is a collaborative, interactive, and systemic experience situated in a given context."

—Michael Fullan, 1993, *Change Forces: Probing the Depths of Educational Reform*, p. 78

We are clearer that the key to student growth is educator growth. They happen together; each enhances the other. Altogether, a "win-win" proposition.

—Bruce Joyce and Beverly Showers, 1995, *Student Achievement Through Staff Development*, p. xv

Adult learning makes a school a learning organization.

—Barbara Gideon and David Erlandson, 2001, *Journal of Staff Development*, p. 16

An alternative high school decided to offer its teachers some specialized training in cooperative learning and multiple intelligences. Afterward they asked the workshop leader to spend several days visiting each classroom to observe the teachers implementing the strategies offered in the training. Time was also provided for the trainer to meet with each teacher individually before and after the classroom observation. The trainer was able to visit each classroom six times, making it possible to ascertain and offer concrete suggestions, then return to watch how the suggestions were implemented. As a result, most of the teachers not only implemented the trainer's suggestions but were pleased that there were real improvements in class responses. The training provided one source for a common understanding to emerge among the faculty. The teacher conferences before and after visits provided another way for common understanding to be expanded. Finally the trainer provided a summary of 10 key strategies that the trainer felt would dramatically improve student learning in this school.

The heart of this section is communication. Understanding what people are saying is fundamental to communication. This chapter is concerned with cognitive connections, with the goal of assuring that everyone's thinking is on the same page. While it may seem that everyone in a school is on the same page, very often what one person means by something means something completely different to the next person. This is why dialogue and study are crucial for making sure that all are operating with a common understanding.

■ A COMMON UNDERSTANDING UNIFIES

Because the United States is a country of one language, it is possible to neglect the crucial role of common understanding. Since the majority of us speak English, we may be misled into thinking that we all know what we mean. That is rarely true even with native English speakers. Add to this the growth in population of people whose native language is not English. Consequently, it is much easier to understand that without a common understanding it is difficult to maintain healthy communication and difficult to avoid misunderstandings. Crucial to building spirit is the capacity and confidence to know what each of us means by what each of us says.

In addition, Jenlink (1995) reminds us that communication is deeply connected to our very thoughts and thinking processes: "Language, thought, and thinking processes are all interwoven into a dynamic that directs individual associations within the complex web of relationships" (Jenlink, 1995, p. 47). Because of this interconnection, common understanding is crucial to giving us windows into what the thoughts and thinking processes are in another.

Whatever change is being attempted in the life of a school, it is important that all understand the language of that change. Concepts need to be clear. The vocabulary connected to the change itself needs to be familiar to all. "Change Axiom: A common change language is essential in matters of creating fundamental change in complex social systems. A common language must be socially constructed, guided by knowledgeable facilitators competent in conventions of change language, and shared on basis of meaning and understanding" (Jenlink, 1995, p. 50). For spirit to grow all this needs to be done early on. "Stakeholder competencies and capacity for creating and sustaining a change conversation through a common change language must be fostered and developed very early in the systemic change process" (Jenlink, 1995, p. 51). Furthermore, this change language needs to be shared in a tone of learning together. Talking down to a group shuts down spirit. "Language is a dynamic cultural artifact that takes an important role in effecting change in complex social systems like education" (Jenlink, 1995, p. 49).

Many teachers from a school on the West Coast attended a workshop led by Dr. Arthur Costa. His work on the 14 intelligent behaviors fascinated them. A few months later, a consultant had the opportunity to work with the faculty on another topic. As this consultant visited each classroom, he was surprised to see posters of all of the 14 intelligent behaviors in every classroom as well as in the hallways. The teachers had developed a common understanding and had decided to make sure teachers and students would benefit from that common understanding every day.

SHARED DATA IS A CRUCIAL STARTING POINT

One helpful starting point in creating a common understanding is shared data. The data start the dialogue process at a very objective place. It is important that the data be used as a source of information and insight rather than as a means of beating people over the head. Rick DuFour treats data as a helpful bridge leading to concerted action. "Using data is the most effective strategy for translating the good intentions described in a vision statement into meaningful school improvement targets" (DuFour, 2000, p. 71). In this way sound data can direct the focus of the vision into strategies that can make a profound difference in the life of a school. Conversations around sound data can pull together people's insights and concerns without getting lost in theory or diverse perspectives.

It is crucial to get as many people as possible involved in studying and interpreting the data. One person or even just a few people will apply only their perspectives on the data. "An organization swimming in many interpretations can then discuss, combine, and build on them. The outcome of such a process has to be a much more diverse and richer sense of what is going on" (Wheatley, 1992, p. 65).

In this way, even in the discussion of the data, bridges and connections can often be made even among those of very differing approaches and viewpoints. Some might raise an objection saying that experts are needed for data analysis and interpretation:

> Educators don't need advanced degrees in statistics to begin gathering and using data in ways that will benefit schools and children. Teachers and school-level administrators can begin by asking questions about student achievement and teaching practice, and gathering many kinds of data so they can answer those questions in a systematic way. (Bernhardt, 2000, p. 36)

Several educators offer ways to question and learn from the data (LeTendre, 2000):

> Getting answers to these questions requires that educators know how to collect, analyze, and interpret data. In other words, they need to know how to conduct a credible program evaluation so that they decide how best to meet the learning needs of all youngsters. Conducting a credible program requires that educators follow six steps:
>
>   1. Pose questions.
>   2. Establish judgment criteria.
>   3. Make a plan.
>   4. Gather data.
>   5. Analyze data.
>   6. Interpret the results. (p. 21)

Note how important it is to begin by asking what you need the data for. This enables a clear focus. There is usually an incredible amount of data available. Knowing your questions can help to prioritize precisely what data are most useful at a given point in time. This is where the judgment criteria come in. Once the questions are posed and the criteria determined, a group can create a plan for the process, including how the data will be gathered. This leaves us with the demanding tasks of analyzing and interpreting the data.

A simple four-tiered question series can help in analyzing data. The four questions are (Pete & Sambo, 2004): What did you find? What else do you know or need to know? What do the data say? What do you need to do now? The first question could include: What data do you particularly recall from your pulling the data together? What data supports what you have experienced, felt, or understood? What data surprised you? The second question could include questions like: What gaps are still present in our data and information? What other questions have arisen seeing the data we now have? How might we procure the additional data and information we need? The third question encompasses questions like: What insights has the data given you? What messages is the data communicating to us? How is the data different from last year's data? Finally, the fourth question could encompass questions like: What are the implications of the data? What are some constructive responses to the data? What practical strategies or approaches would increase student learning and achievement given the data we now have?

Wheatley encourages a constant influx of new data so that an organization can be made even more responsive (Wheatley, 1992, p. 107). For Wheatley it is as if information is the lifeblood of a dynamic, healthy organization (Wheatley, 1992, p. 105). What is crucial is how the information is used. Just dumping data onto staff people has only limited impact. Holding structured conversations to find the meaning in the data really provides the lifeblood. Indeed it is through such conversations and discussions that powerful insights and connections can emerge, insights and connections that can lead to solid innovations (Wheatley, 1992, p. 113). The process of moving from data, to insights and connections, to solid innovations can be powerful and motivating for staff. This process can become the heart of effective staff development.

"We emphasize the conduct of staff development as inquiry (continuous data collection, analysis, and interpretation) even more than we did a few years ago" (Joyce & Showers, 1995, p. xv).

We know that in the classroom one effective strategy is problem-based learning. Giving students a complex and maybe even unclear problem to research draws their curiosity into research, clear problem formulation, and alternative solutions. This can work for staff too. When this process is carried out well, the involvement increases and the spirit runs high.

> A school district in the South had become very committed to working with data. They made sure that their teachers all became proficient at gathering and analyzing data from their students' performance. More than that, this district decided that all students also needed to become adept at gathering, tracking, and analyzing their own data. Consequently, each teacher made sure that students had charts and tools to track the data from their own tests, projects, and performances. Much to the teachers' surprise, the students became quite involved and excited about tracking their own data.

COMMON STUDY CREATES MIND CONNECTIONS

Common study is one way to bring people together and deepen their connections to each other with common understanding. In other words, this is one way that can lead to enhancing the spirit in a school when done well. Senge likes to refer to this result as an "alignment." As this alignment deepens, groups also deepen their ability to think dynamically (Senge, Kleiner, Roberts, Ross, & Smith, 1994, p. 352). When this happens an atmosphere of openness and support is created that can foster courage and risk.

"A critical finding was that the climate of support, combined with a commitment to learning together, generated a more, rather than less, questioning approach to improvement, and more rather than less risk-taking" (Fullan, 1993, p. 63). This suggests that the climate of support and common study can create the lively, dynamic, spirit-filled environment that fosters a willingness to try new things on behalf of enhancing student learning and achievement.

In addition, there is another effect of this connecting of the minds. It builds a confidence that something can be done. It builds a confidence to pursue grand yet realistic schemes to counteract some of the many blocks to student achievement and learning.

A related effect of this common study is what it does to build a community of learners. In other words, students, teachers, and administrators are all together on a path of discovery. Simply put, when educators grow, students grow (Joyce & Showers, 1995, p. xv). This suggests that the reason common study is so dynamic and effective is because the learnings of the teacher and the student impact each other.

"Without exception, intellectual stimulation is a burning need of the teachers I interviewed" (Williams, J. S., 2003, p. 72). This suggests that our teachers are eager, if not even starving, for the kind of stimulation that quality common study can afford. It is this very common study that can grow a staff eager for the task of teaching and competent in the challenges faced every day.

■ COMMON UNDERSTANDING LEADS TO MORAL PURPOSE

It is only through deep study and profound dialogue that a group can finally evolve its moral purpose. By moral purpose, I am not referring to any particular religious doctrine or prescript. By moral purpose, I am referring to the underlying reason why an educational institution exists. There is no question, especially in this rapidly changing technological, cybernetic age, that crucial information and concepts are needed to be fully educated in this century. That alone, however, will not create men and women who are thoughtful, ethical citizens of the world. That is where moral purpose comes in. Perhaps moral purpose gets taught more by how an educator acts and behaves than by anything particular that is said. Profound regard for life, living life on behalf of others, and appreciating beauty are all pieces of what we also want to convey to students beyond information, facts, details, and concepts.

First, teachers of the future will make their commitment to moral purpose—making a difference in the lives of children—more prominent, more active, more visible, and more problematic. Many teachers have moral purpose now, but they do not conceptualize it that way. They do not give themselves the stature they deserve. They must push moral purpose to the forefront, but along with other components. . . . Otherwise it leads to frustration, burnout, cynicism or moral martyrdom. (Fullan, 1993, p. 80)

Surely some of the frustration, burnout, and cynicism many of our teachers experience are related to the prevalence of unacknowledged or unarticulated deep moral purpose in our learning communities. In our rush to prepare students to do well on standardized tests, teachers, students, and administrators easily lose sight of the very reasons many entered into the difficult and demanding world of education. Especially in schools where test scores are consistently difficult to raise, it is very easy for teachers to become demoralized—that is totally losing sight of the deep moral purpose of education.

Fullan does not beat around the bush: "Scratch a good teacher and you will find a moral purpose" (Fullan, 1993, p. 10). It is the moral purpose that is fundamentally underneath the drive to become a good teacher. Likewise, it is the moral purpose in a learning community that enables it to become a spirit-filled community. "If concerns for making a difference remain at the one-to-one and classroom level, it cannot be done. An additional component is required. Making a difference must be explicitly recast in broader social and moral terms" (Fullan, 1993, p. 11). Through common understanding, the possibility of moral purpose, of seriously making a difference can transform the entire learning community.

What keeps really great teachers in the classroom? If you ask them, they will not mention salary, benefits, working conditions, power, or prestige. These 12 exemplary teachers say that they have been able to fulfill strong personal needs for autonomy and creativity in their classrooms, and their rewards are meaningful relationships and the knowledge that they are making a difference in the lives of students. (Williams, J. S., 2003, p. 74)

Howard Gardner articulates that from his perspective education would do better to focus less time on facts, less time on lots of information, and more time on what he calls "the True, the Beautiful, and the Good" (Gardner, 2000, p. 16). Certainly if education totally misses these three, it is not adequately preparing men and women to be thoughtful global citizens.

COMMON, PURPOSEFUL GOALS ■ BUILD ON INDIVIDUAL GOALS

When the study and research reaches a certain point, it is time to fashion the direction of the school and, then, the direction of professional development. It is at this point that the wise leader helps the group to blend individual goals, state mandates, and district directions into school-specific common goals.

No longer can we assume people will blindly follow whatever abstract goals are suggested from "on high." Passion for common goals is built on the passion each person has for individual goals. The route to common goals requires that individual goals pass through common understanding. Common goals have a better chance of succeeding when each person sees how the common goals assist reaching individual goals. "Adults engaged in learning and change have common needs. They need to be exposed to new and innovative ideas that are relevant to their personal and professional concerns" (Nevills, 2003, p. 23). In other words, one taps into the passion for individual goals to build passion for the common goal. Individuals need to see how their individual goals are furthered or included within the common goal. This happens by building connections through common understandings.

To build these common connections, teachers need to begin by thinking through what their professional goals are for their careers; what their hopes and aspirations are for their own teaching and their growth. Without that thinking, there can't be any fruitful dialogue with the federal and state mandates as well as the district goals. With that thinking, a group will be better able to fashion the school-specific goals. Following that, there needs to be study and dialogue to assist the move from individual goals to common goals.

Bellanca notes Fullan's wisdom in linking professional development with personal development. "Most importantly, Fullan should be credited for his leadership in challenging educators to connect personal development to organizational development" (Bellanca, 1995, p. 15). These are not two distinct areas. For both to work, they both need to be interrelated and supportive of each other.

■ PARTICIPATION AND SHARED DECISION MAKING FORM A PLANNED, COMPREHENSIVE PROFESSIONAL DEVELOPMENT SYSTEM

Chapter 1 makes clear that in this age participation is crucial. Furthermore, shared decision making is the necessary vehicle for getting things accomplished in schools. This also holds true for professional development systems. The era of centrally planned, top-down professional development is now being complemented by faculty decision making on what professional development makes sense at the local school level. A critical element in shared decision making is that the necessary information is shared broadly and effectively.

Joyce and Showers (1995) suggest that when 80 percent of the faculty agree on a professional development direction with the stipulation that once decided all will support it, very little conflict over that decision follows (Joyce & Showers, 1995, p. 14).

Bellanca helpfully outlines the distinction among inservices, staff development, and professional development systems (Bellanca, 1995, p. 6). Inservices are often full-day or half-day awareness workshops that acquaint staff with some new direction or way of teaching. As he points out, very often these times are mandated institute days that are often preceded by a frantic search for someone who can deliver the inservice.

Staff development is often orchestrated at the district level. A particular teaching need may be the basis for choosing what staff development to offer. It is hoped that this blanket approach will fulfill and meet that need broadly. In this way, the district approach will hit both those who need it and those who don't. Hence many teachers look down on staff development as wasted time.

A professional development system is planned, systemic, and comprehensive. It is more an alternate way of doing staff development in that it emphasizes opportunities for both individual pursuit of professional development goals and schoolwide professional development, which speaks to a particular direction the school wants to emphasize or speaks to a teaching need in the school (identified, perhaps, by test data analysis). The school's direction of professional development encourages teachers to create their own professional development goals. Then they are held accountable for the completion of these goals within their planned time frame. This puts professional development responsibility on all teachers, whether they are brand new to teaching or whether they have had 25 years of experience. With a combination of individual professional development and school-specific professional development, the heart and the power of the professional development system happen within the individual school, for the school is where the unique directions are formulated for which professional development is needed. When this is allowed to occur, great faculty energy can be generated both toward professional development and toward its transference into the classroom.

Needless to say, one of the biggest questions raised relative to all of this is how to find the time to allow this approach to happen. Yet, today professional development is not an extra. If educational institutions are to realize the demands put on them, there must be time carved out for this. For Joyce and Showers, that time has to be included in the time flow of a normal workday (Joyce & Showers, 1995, p. xvi). In no way is this going to be easy given the current way an average school day is carried out today.

When it becomes obvious to the school that a training session is needed, Joyce and Showers (1995) give clear direction on four crucial components of the training. The first component delivers the basic theory and direction, clarifying the need as well as the theory and the research behind the theory. The second component is a demonstration or modeling of the recommended action or format for the classroom. The third component is a time for practice in as realistic a setting as possible. The fourth component is peer coaching. More has been said about peer coaching in Chapter 1.

PRACTICE WITH PEERS AND IN THE CLASSROOM TO BRING ABOUT INSTRUCTIONAL CHANGE

Common understanding continues to grow and develop as teachers put into practice the results of their research, study, and training. Connections grow even deeper as teachers have a chance to implement what they've learned. As stated previously, practice is one part of effective professional development. The first component of this practice is with peers. A lot of fear and roughness can be smoothed out with some amount of practice in front of peers before moving into a classroom setting. This is an absolutely crucial stage if there is any desire for training to move into the classroom.

The research that Joyce and Showers (1995) have done over the last two decades indicates that this collegial opportunity for practice is a mandatory step for teachers to make the aspects of the training their own.

Black (2003) elucidates a further importance of allowing not only time for practice but also time for reflecting on that practice:

> To become proficient, teachers, like doctors, need time to practice and refine new strategies and techniques. And they need time to reflect, learn from mistakes, and work with colleagues as they acquire good judgment and tacit knowledge about classroom teaching and learning. The question facing schools is how to find time for teachers to practice what they learn in courses, workshops, training sessions, and other staff development programs. The training-learning process all takes time. Yet time is what it takes to create teachers who genuinely absorb and put into use whatever training has occurred. Imagine the excitement generated in a staff that discovers the efficacy of new ways of teaching, of experiencing firsthand responses from their students not thought possible before. (p.12)

The four-component training process we've discussed calls into question one standard way staff development has been done heretofore. A one-hour, two-hour, half-day, or even full-day staff development session that does not include demonstration and time for practice is really cheating the teachers of their opportunity, indeed their right, to expand their teaching repertoires and skills.

■ ACTIVITY TEN—ILLUMINATE CRUCIAL DATA

Description

Data are often boring or overwhelming. Helping the staff make sense of data can help the staff focus on what is going on and how to make improvements. Two tools can help do this. One is a data screen. The other is a series of questions for everyone to ask about the data.

Methodology

1. A data screen has various categories into which data can be placed. Using the data screen, have teams put as much data as they can in the various screen boxes.

2. Go around and have teams share some of the data in each of the screen boxes.

3. Ask the teams what data stand out; for example, what data seem particularly important or relevant?

4. Ask the teams which data surprised them or confirmed an intuition.

5. Ask the teams what relationships and connections they see among the different screen boxes.

6. Ask the teams what all this is telling them; for example, what messages are the data sending?

7. Finally, what are some implications or next steps to take relative to the data?

8. Pete and Sambo (p. 43) also suggest four key questions:
   a. What data do we have?
   b. What else do we know or need to know?
   c. So, what inferences can we make?
   d. Now, what do you need to do?

Example

Table 3.1 is a data screen to hold information about the school and the community. Template 10 provides a blank of the data screen.

There are five categories in this data screen example. Perhaps all of them aren't needed. Perhaps others are needed. The crucial point is the usefulness of a data screen as opposed to three or more pages of data listings.

Metacognitive Insights

Pages and pages of data are overwhelming. It is impossible to absorb what the data communicate. Organizing the data in a data screen allows people to grasp the meaning behind the data as well as begin to discern relationships and connections among the data.

A key trait of the leader at this point is the trust the leader puts toward the teams studying the data. While any one person might not see the whole picture, a team together can often generate very accurate and perceptive insights about the data.

ACTIVITY ELEVEN—GATHER RELEVANT RESEARCH ■

Description

In addition to data from the school and from the community, it is crucial to keep up with relevant research. However, that can be a daunting task for staff that is already feeling overwhelmed with everyday school tasks. There needs to be a simple way to tap the wisdom from the many books and articles that are available. That is why this activity provides a simple form that a person or a team could use to share some of the important insights from research. Would it be possible then for some of this to be shared in five minutes during regular staff meetings? Up to now, most schools depend on teachers to keep abreast of educational happenings on their own. Think of the richness that could occur if research reports were woven into the regular staff or department meetings.

Methodology

Individuals or teams are given a book or an article on which to make a report.

Table 3.1   Data Screen

Education Indicators
Graduation rates
State test scores
Teacher's formal education levels
Absenteeism figures
Student mobility rates

Economic Indicators
Average community household income
Poverty rates
% of students on free or reduced lunch
% of substandard housing

Home Life Indicators
% of dual-parent and single-parent homes of students
% of homes where another language is spoken
Number of foster care placements
Immunization rates for young children
Reported cases of abuse and neglect

Community Life Indicators
Demographics of community
Number of social and community organizations
Number of religious institutions
Voter participation rates

Employment Indicators
Number of businesses in town
Number of large businesses
Community unemployment rate
% of postsecondary and college-bound high school graduates
Kinds of businesses that are hiring

1. Several elements are necessary for the brief research report. Whether it is a book or an article, there needs to be a summary of three to five key insights chosen from the material by the reviewer.

2. The reader needs to reflect on why these insights are important or how these insights are relevant to the staff at the school.

3. The reader needs to create examples of how the insights could be applied in the local school's situation.

4. The reader needs to suggest some questions gleaned from reading the book or article.

Example

Table 3.2 offers an example of a brief research analysis report. Template 11 provides a blank of this resource analysis form.

Table 3.2   Resource Analysis

Author's insights	1. Four key frames: political, Human Resources, structural, and symbolic.
	2. Most educators rely on the Human Resources and the structural frames.
	3. Conflict can be a source of energy and renewal.
	4. The symbolic frame is the doorway to dynamic schools.
Reflections	1. These frames could be used for analysis of school problems.
	2. Most educators need tools to help a group work through conflict.
	3. Some leaders and schools are afraid of the symbolic.
Questions	1. How can the symbolic frame be made to come alive for educators?
	2. What skills are useful for each of the frames?

SOURCE: Bolman, L. G., & Deal, T. E. (2002). *Reframing the path to school leadership* (pp. 3–4, 51–53, 104–105). Thousand Oaks, CA: Corwin.

Metacognitive Insights

If we expect our students to grow and learn, staff needs to model growing and learning. Staff needs to find simple ways to keep their own minds thinking and growing. This activity helps the group's mind to stretch and grow. In addition, it enhances common understanding among the staff.

ACTIVITY TWELVE—FOSTER ■
FIFTEEN-MINUTE COMMON STUDIES

Description

Teachers who are actively expanding their knowledge of their content area or grade-level area model the active learning mind to their students.

Consequently, this activity suggests a mere 15 minutes out of a department-level meeting or grade-level meeting be devoted to a brief common study. It involves only one teacher at a time preparing a short presentation followed by application. In this way minds are stimulated and the insights from individual professional study can become whole-group learning.

Methodology

1. The basis of this 15-minute common study can be a short article. I suggest an article as opposed to a book, as teachers are busy and pressed for time.

2. Cull out the key points, especially those with relatively easy transfer to the classrooms of teachers in the group.

3. Choose an image that helps to pull these insights together.

4. Add any necessary supporting details.

5. Pick a lesson or unit to model the transfer of the insights.

6. Choose a question to catalyze application thinking for the teachers.

7. Allow some time for questions, issues, or concerns.

Table 3.3 offers a time flow design for a 15-minute study format for reporting on an article or book reviewed.

Table 3.3   Fifteen-Minute Common Study Format

Part One: Five Minutes	Part Two: Seven Minutes	Part Three: Three Minutes
Overview	Applications	Questions, issues, concerns

Example

Overview

Table 3.4 offers the four insights from Claudia Wallis related to the cognitive abilities of adolescent brains and how adults can respond appropriately.

Application

1. Describe a lesson that involves challenge and risk taking for the students with an opportunity for independence but with clear structure. Ask the group to share another example.

2. Ask the group what implications come to them from this article.

Questions, Issues, Concerns

This is an opportunity for the teachers to ask questions or raise concerns they have relative to the practical application of the ideas presented.

Table 3.4   Four Main Points

1. Adolescents' brains are not fully developed. They have a relatively small amount of cognitive control. Final brain development, the ability to make reasoned decisions, occurs early in one's 20s.

4. Hints—Good parenting and good teaching make a difference: Give appropriate praise, set limits, provide structure, encourage appropriate independence, explain decisions.

2. Raging hormones lead to thrill seeking and risk taking when good judgment is weak.

"What makes teens tick."

3. Good judgment alone does not mean good judgment in a group.

SOURCE: From Wallis, C. (2004, May 10). What makes teens tick. *Time 163*(9), 56–65.

Metacognitive Insights

This short study format can help to take away the tendency for meetings to be focused only on bureaucratic concerns. This format, when done regularly, provides a pointed reminder that teaching involves continual learning. Imagine the effect if these studies happened even every other week during the school year. That could mean perhaps 15 or more such brief studies.

ACTIVITY THIRTEEN—SET UP   ■
FOCUSED WHOLE-SCHOOL TRAINING

Description

Whole-school formal inservice training needs to be aligned to the particular school's instructional emphases. In other words, training sessions need to complement the school's mission and its particular goals. Training needs to come out of staff-identified goals and training needs. Ideally, training is much more than a one-shot session. An afternoon or even a day-long workshop only barely gets the staff familiar with the concept being taught. Much more is needed, including peer coaching, if the training is to reach the classroom.

Methodology

The following training flow for each session is helpful:

1. Context—This can be a reminder of the process and decision that determined what training would be offered to the staff.

2. Need—Some attention needs to be paid as to why this training is being offered in the first place. This is where some research data and, better yet, local data substantiate the need for the training. In addition, projection of what the results could be for the staff, the students, indeed for the whole school would be beneficial.

3. Direct teaching—Whatever the topic, there needs to be some form of input offered. This could take the form of brief lectures, presentations, videos, articles, or firsthand experiences from teachers who have used whatever the training is about.

4. Actual practice—At some point in effective training there needs to be some actual practice done by the participants—the staff needs to begin directly applying the content of the training in some practical way. A nonthreatening environment encourages staff to take more risks here.

5. Monitoring—During this practice and application time, the training presenter should monitor how the practice is going. Moving from group to group allows a training presenter to check on how well the practice is going. Very often as the presenter moves around, groups who might be hesitant to ask a question in the whole-group setting will feel free to get clarification within their small group.

6. Follow-up plan—There are several ways to implement follow-up to these sessions. A follow-up training date could be established to add additional input relative to the training topic or to hear reports of how the implementation is going in the classroom. Teachers might bring a concrete product from an activity used to implement the training topic in the classroom. A video camera can document how some teachers have implemented the training. A small portion of regularly scheduled staff meetings could be used to hear how implementation is going. Administration can make implementation of this training a clear part of their administrative evaluations of each teacher. Finally, another follow-up approach can be peer coaching.

7. Processing—Each training session needs to conclude with some form of reflection on the key topics or noted experiences of the training. Questions like: What will you remember next week about this training today? What were several of the big ideas or big themes of our training? What worked for you today in terms of how we did this training?

Example

Table 3.5 offers an example of a training session using these seven parts. Template 12 provides a blank form for planning a training session.

Table 3.5 An Awareness Session on Multiple Intelligences (MI)

Flow	Content
Context	Staff decision to study MI
Need	Diverse abilities in students
Direct teaching	MI theory
Actual practice	MI activities and lesson planning
Monitoring	Leader observation and lesson sharing
Follow-up plan	Class artifact for next session
Processing	Concepts learned; how they impact teaching

Metacognitive Insights

Because there often is so much that an administrative leader wants the teachers to know, many small training sessions on different topics are scheduled throughout the year. This does not really get the material into the classroom. It is more helpful to focus training sessions that might continue for the whole year. That is why in this case "Less is more."

It is helpful to offer the staff several different ways to implement a training topic. Some teachers will immediately want to implement the whole show. Others may feel comfortable implementing small pieces at a time. Suggesting different levels of implementation may help those less adventurous to begin some form of implementation. Affirming all these levels helps get more teachers on board.

ACTIVITY FOURTEEN—IMPLEMENT ACTION RESEARCH PROJECTS

Description

Action research projects may sound intimidating. However, they can be rewarding ways to improve teaching skills and increase confidence.

> . . . action research is a methodology through which teachers can formulate a research question that is central to their own professional practice, devise methods of collecting data pertinent to the question, enact the data collection, analyze the data, articulate the findings and conclusions that inform their teaching practice, and then change their teaching in ways indicated by the research findings and conclusions. (Marshak, 1997, p. 9)

The underlying purpose of this process is to enable the improvement of the whole learning environment. Furthermore, the entire process puts teachers in the driver's seat to examine issues and concerns they have encountered. While it is possible to create a very complex process, perhaps even using sophisticated data collection and analyzing techniques, the purpose here is to reveal a simple process structure that can make action research a possibility for any teacher.

Note the difference between traditional academic research and the action research being implemented by many teachers today.

"The purpose of conventional academic research most often is to develop and articulate knowledge" (Marshak, 1997, p. 24).

"Action research, in contrast, is focused on identifying problems of practice and solving problems and improving practice" (Marshak, 1997, p. 25).

Academic research is often out to generate the kind of knowledge that will lead to broad generalizations and principles. A teacher's action research, on the other hand, is very specific and is only looking for results that will affect the teacher's practice in the classroom. Consequently, the teacher needs only enough data to assist in affirming a teaching practice or to assist in modifying or eliminating a teaching practice.

Methodology

Marshak (1997, pp. 11–18) helps us greatly by providing four basic steps with an optional fifth step:

1. State the issue, concern, or challenge and discern the key research question. (This may include pulling together some relevant research.)

2. Create appropriate research instruments or tools for the data.

3. Gather the data, give the data some organization, discern the insights from the data, and pull out some appropriate conclusions.

4. Develop an action plan to put the findings into practice.

5. (Optional) Share your findings.

Table 3.6 offers a guideline for proceeding through the process of the action research project.

Example

1. My research question: How will using students' own formulated questions about an upcoming unit impact their motivation and willingness to learn?

2. My research tool: A research tool provides a mechanism to help answer the research question, such as illustrated in Table 3.7.

3. Focus on the data: The data have been quite well organized because of the organization of the research tool. The findings are dramatic. Beginning a unit with the students' own formulated questions

Table 3.6   Simple Action Research Plan

Flow	Items to Consider
Research question	Name the issue or concern. Carry out initial brief research. Develop the research question.
Research instrument	Discern the kind of data that will be most useful in answering the research question. Develop the tool or instrument that will hold the data.
Focus on the data	Gather the data. Discover patterns or relationships in the data. Formulate conclusions or findings from the data.
Action plan	State the implications of the researched information relative to the research question. Use the implications to complete an action plan putting the findings into practice.
Share findings	Share the findings through a simple verbal or written report to the faculty. Write an article for an educational journal. Present the findings at a national or regional conference.

positively impacted the process of learning, the sources of research used, the quality of their final report, and their attendance and tardiness. The classes all felt very focused and dynamic as students carried out their research and even talked on task to other students to get help. Table 3.8 is the same research tool with the research results included.

4. Action plan: It takes a lot of time to organize a student-question–driven unit. My goal is to create such units and interject them in an every-other-unit schedule for the rest of the year, with the hope that next year at least two thirds of my units will be student-question driven.

5. Share the findings: The principal has allowed me 10 minutes at the next faculty meeting to go over my action research project and share the results.

Metacognitive Insights

The gift of action research is that teacher-generated questions, derived from the teacher's practical teaching experience, can be a tremendous motivating factor in engaging the teacher in action research. The focus of such research is always to improve teaching skills and student achievement. If even half of the faculty engaged in this, imagine the continuous improvement that would be occurring in the school.

Table 3.7   Research Tool

Category	Previous Unit With Teacher-Formulated Questions	Current Unit With Student-Formulated Questions
Time on task in the classroom		
Homework		
Number of research sources		
Attendance		
Tardiness		
Average rubric grade for final report		

Table 3.8   Research Tool With Accumulated Information

Category	Previous Unit With Teacher-Formulated Questions	Current Unit With Student-Formulated Questions
Time on task in the classroom	60% time on task.	85% time on task.
Homework	50% of homework assignments turned in.	75% of homework assignments turned in.
Number of research sources	Average for each student was two sources.	Average for each student was 10 sources.
Attendance	An average of four student absences per week.	An average of two student absences per week.
Tardiness	An average of three tardinesses per week.	An average of one tardiness per week.
Average rubric grade for final report	78.	86.

4

Leading Guided Reflections

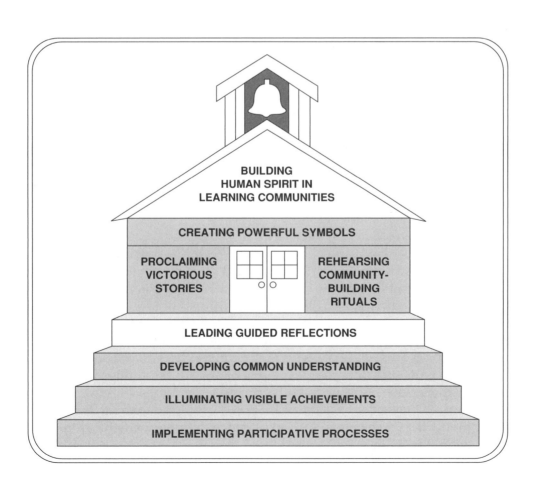

BUILDING
HUMAN SPIRIT IN
LEARNING COMMUNITIES

CREATING POWERFUL SYMBOLS

PROCLAIMING
VICTORIOUS
STORIES

REHEARSING
COMMUNITY-
BUILDING
RITUALS

LEADING GUIDED REFLECTIONS

DEVELOPING COMMON UNDERSTANDING

ILLUMINATING VISIBLE ACHIEVEMENTS

IMPLEMENTING PARTICIPATIVE PROCESSES

But if people were to think together in a coherent way, it would have tremendous power. If there was an opportunity for sustained dialogue over a period of time, we would have coherent movement of thought, not only at the conscious level which we all recognize, but even more importantly at the tacit level, the unspoken level which cannot be described.

—Joseph Jaworski, 1996, *Synchronicity: The Inner Path of Leadership* (p. 111)

A private school for middle school and high school students overhauled its focus and curricula and offered updated teacher training to become a "world academy." This process took several years. Each year the faculty reflected back on the previous year and initiated detailed planning for the next year. The facilitator noted the four broad strategies that had been decided on the year before. Then he had the faculty brainstorm as many events, happenings, successes, and victories as they could come up with. The faculty wrote these on separate pieces of paper and put them up on a wall close to the strategy they were most closely associated with. The facilitator had them all stand close to the wall for a short reflective conversation. He began asking them to call out events and happenings that were particularly noticeable on the wall. He then asked which ones they were particularly pleased with or proud of. Following that, they shared ones that were relatively easy to pull off and ones that were much more difficult to accomplish. The group then shared the different place they now thought the school was in given all of the recorded happenings. They wrapped up the conversation by articulating the major concepts and applications learned during the past year and shared their insights about significant implications for the next step of their planning. Many of the faculty expressed gratitude for the opportunity to step back and note the successes as well as reflect on the importance of what they had accomplished.

The previous chapter dealt a great deal with cognition. This chapter delves into the metacognition or deep reflection. If the goal of Chapter 3 is to get everyone "on the same page," then the goal of this chapter is to explore ways of binding people together in more ways than the cognitive. One might say that the binding occurs more through connecting feelings, hearts, and shared experiences.

Senge likes to refer to this result as an "alignment." As this alignment deepens, groups also deepen their ability to think dynamically (Senge, Kleiner, Roberts, Ross, & Smith, 1994, p. 352). Senge's use of the word alignment is significant here. The alignment he suggests is far more than an alignment of ideas. He suggests that this alignment brings connections of people's hearts as well as their minds. This alignment comes not just from studying and sharing ideas but from sharing teaching experiences and life experiences; it comes when individuals share their commitments and their passions; it comes when people of very different viewpoints discover deep human connections with each other; it comes when people are able to share what is deeply significant and meaningful to them. It is at this point that spirit comes alive. This experience only happens when people share deeply and freely.

When team learning becomes more than just an intellectual exercise, emotional, social, and spirit connections can happen. This calls for the kind of leadership that is always ready with questions that help the group delve into their deep thinking and feeling, thus ending up sharing in a way much more profound than merely studying facts, information, tools, and concepts.

Guided reflections happen through journal writing and through reflective conversations/discussions. Opportunities for quiet journal writing give the writer a chance to pay attention to deeper thoughts or deeper voices inside—a chance for those thoughts and voices to be recognized and articulated. Sometimes it is only in moments like these that connections are seen for the very first time. Sometimes it is only in moments like these that solutions to a nagging issue are suddenly discerned. Yet the very fast-paced school schedules and tightly-packed personal lives experienced by many educators make this time for reflection difficult to realize.

A HELPFUL ENVIRONMENT ENHANCES INDIVIDUAL JOURNAL WRITING

Some people find that individual reflective time happens in the car as they ride to and return from work. Consciously or unconsciously, they may carry out questions like those posed in Activity Fifteen. Other people find that actually writing things down is the most effective way to reflect. Occasionally a team leader, a department chair, or a school administrator may structure reflective writing into regularly scheduled meetings. This is probably rare.

The following are clues that support an environment of successful individual journal writing. Relative quiet allows the person to focus attention on the writing. A moment that is relatively free of distractions also encourages reflection. Some teachers use a few minutes in the classroom after school has been dismissed. A small notebook devoted only to this journaling is a tangible way to say to the unconscious that this activity is important. Some people find that a particular small picture helps them to focus their energies on reflection. A consistent time to reflect and write helps make journal writing a habit. Some find that quiet background music adds to the environment. Some like to read an uplifting few sentences or an inspiring quote to help them focus. Even four or five minutes at a time can make a huge difference. As all of this is individual and personal, each person needs to explore and experiment with the environment that most helps that person to reflect and write.

Several consultants when charging participants to implement something new in the classroom suggest they create a double-entry journal. The left half of the journal page includes reflections before, during, and right after the lesson. Then the right half of the journal page is for reflections three or four days later. Often the right side of the journal page is filled with concerns about whether the strategy to be implemented will be successful or not. Also the right side documents some

(Continued)

(Continued)

of the steps taken to prepare for the implementation. The left side is often filled with great pride and satisfaction that the strategy worked. In addition, the left side often has ideas to improve the next implementation of the strategy. Teachers comment about how helpful it is to add reflections three or four days after implementation. Sometimes initial concerns that a lesson did not turn out well prove to be mistaken, and this insight can only be discovered after a few days. Teachers also like to document steps taken ahead of time, as that provides guidelines for the future implementation of new strategies.

ACTIVITY FIFTEEN—ENCOURAGE INDIVIDUAL JOURNAL WRITING

Description

This activity provides some structural guidelines to help one begin writing in a journal. Just as with students, often particular questions help to stir thinking. Others may feel very comfortable writing in a "stream of consciousness" flow.

Methodology

1. Follow the same structure as that suggested for conversations: data, feelings, interpretation, and next steps or decisions. In this flow the questions might be:
   a. What happened? What led up to what happened?
   b. What are my feelings about what happened? What feelings did others have?
   c. Why did this happen? What did I learn from what happened?
   d. What changes need to be made? How might I operate differently?

2. Another set of questions might be:
   a. What was my plan?
   b. What went well?
   c. What would I do differently next time?
   d. What assistance do I need?

Example

What happened? What led up to what happened?—I was teaching one of my favorite lessons. Since I was in high school this part of history has always fascinated me. Half way through the lesson, suddenly Mario said quite loudly, "This is boring. Why do I have to learn this?" I admit that I was shocked. How could anyone not find all of what I was talking about fascinating? I abruptly asked Mario to be quiet and continued to teach. In about three minutes, Shirley interrupted me saying, "Mario is right. This is boring." I was so upset that I stopped teaching and had everyone read the chapter in the history text until the bell rang.

What are my feelings about what happened?—I was shocked and angry. I was really furious that Mario piped up with his comment. Then I got further irate when Shirley affirmed what Mario had said.

Why did it happen? What did I learn from what happened?—As I reflect on this, I was already upset this morning when I arrived at school and learned we had an afterschool meeting just when I had arranged to meet a friend right after school. I also believe I could have asked Mario and Shirley some questions to probe what exactly was boring to them. Now that I think about this, I did nothing to relate my history lesson to something the students could identify with.

What changes will I make? One of the major themes of this history lesson is how people rebelled and revolted against rulers they thought were unjust and unfair. I could begin this lesson by asking them when they have felt they had been treated unjustly and unfairly. Then I could ask them how they dealt with that. With that context, I could begin my history lesson from an entirely different perspective.

Metacognitive Insights

Some people write in journals every day. Others write only occasionally. Some write about the very ordinary happenings of a day. Others write about specific events—either out of joy and pride or out of struggle and frustration. The key is to discover what works for the particular person.

SKILLFULLY LED CONVERSATIONS ■

Skillfully led conversations are not just ordinary conversations; they are highly structured. With adept facilitators, these conversations enhance the reflective processes of the group and increase their collective capabilities; they bring about increased energy, spirit, and courage; they help a group to listen carefully for an emerging whole picture; and they occasion deep reflection. Because of all of these benefits, skillfully led conversations put powerful chinks in an environment of isolation.

A presenter has frequently used the "Why I'm in Teaching" conversation in Activity Twenty-One. Without fail, teachers love hearing other teachers talk about high points in their careers. However, a special bond occurs when teachers talk about the low points. All the participants identify with those. When teachers start to talk about why they still continue to teach, the room always gets quiet. Sometimes they refer to the commitment to follow in a revered teacher's footsteps. Sometimes they remind themselves of a student whose life they touched. Sometimes they remind themselves of their decision to care for students, to make a difference for the future. Whether they talk out loud or are silent, everyone is exploring why he or she comes

(Continued)

(Continued)

to school every day and works with the students. This kind conversation touches more than the mind. It impacts the hearts of all the participants.

Skillfully Led Conversations Enhance the Reflective Processes and Collective Capabilities

When conversations are well-led, the ability of a group to think and reflect together is dramatically enhanced. Reflective processes will deepen. Also, there will be shifts in what the group is thinking. This may happen without people being very consciously aware of the change. In other words, such conversations can change the very thinking capacity, reflecting capacity, learning capacity, and communication capacity (Nelson, 2001, pp. 2–7).

When conversations are skillfully led, people discover that they don't have to agree with or like everything that is said. They are only called on to pay attention to what is said. By paying attention, they may be able to discern an action that will make sense to everyone. This kind of conversation is very demanding. It takes work to be attentive. The promise is the potential of the release of a great deal of power. "When people sit in dialogue together, they are exercising leadership as a whole. This is nothing less than the unfolding of the generative process. It's the way that thought participates in creating, but it can only be done collectively" (Jaworski, 1996, p. 116). In addition, there is a way that skillfully led conversation can lead to great creativity because it is tapping the mind of the group in a different way than in everyday conversational encounters. Because of this, there is a potential for a deep trust to emerge in the group (Fullan & Hargreaves, 1996, p. 74). An appreciation emerges for the gifts of those participating in the conversation.

Skillfully Led Conversations Bring About Energy, Spirit, and Courage

While skillfully led conversations intensify the reflecting processes of a group, they also infuse energy, spirit, and courage. Perhaps that energy comes from a deeper sense of connection among those in the group. "In dialogue, the goal is to create a special environment in which a different kind of relationship among parts can come into play—one that reveals both high energy and high intelligence" (Jaworski, 1996, p. 111). In other words, it is possible for dialogue to transport people to a different kind of experience that occasions the appearance of new energy, new spirit, and new courage. To bring this life into the learning community, it is necessary to begin talking about matters of spirit—topics not generally considered in a time when there is such exclusive focus on content (information, concepts, and, of course, test scores). "We learned how the isolation of individuals—the taboo against talking about spiritual matters in the public sphere—robs people of courage, of the strength of heart to do what deep down they believe to be right. They think they are alone in facing these issues" (Bolman & Deal, 2002, p. 3). When structured conversations are well led, people are permitted to come face to face with deep concerns and profound resolve. When this happens, people view each other with new respect and even new delight.

"A conversation with several people can generate commitment, bond a team, generate new options, or build a vision. Conversations can shift working patterns, build friendships, create focus and energy, cement resolve" (Stanfield, 1997, p. 6).

Without paying attention to these matters, organizations, schools, and teams fall into a spiritless, humdrum, unmotivated environment that eats away at whatever deep purposes brought people into learning communities in the first place. "If we do not listen to the spirit within us, our deepest longings go unfulfilled" (Bolman & Deal, 2002, p. 4).

Skillfully Led Conversations Enable Listening for the Underlying Whole

When working with a group, it is helpful to rehearse that the intent is not to make a particular person's idea visible to the group. Rather it is to make the thinking of the whole group visible to itself. The task in a conversation is "allowing the whole that exists to become manifest" (Jaworski, p. 116). It is this very "whole" that enables a group to feel its connections with one another and to feel previous barriers breaking down.

"If ten people are conversing around a table, the truth lies not with any one of them, but in the centre of the table, between and among the perspectives of all ten" (Stanfield, 1997, p. 10).

When this kind of listening occurs, unifying forces are encouraged and begin to deepen the group's sense of empowerment and efficacy.

Skillfully Led Conversations Provide Chinks in the Environment of Isolation

School schedules are often so hectic and overloaded that there is little time for significant conversations and connections to happen during the school day. Isolation from other teachers is the unintended norm in schools. Consequently, it becomes more crucial than ever to provide opportunities for teachers to connect. Administrators and teachers alike are hungry for conversations that go much farther than the latest concern or bureaucratic mandate. Their minds are thirsting for conversations that help them connect to others through common purposes, common values, and common experiences. Periodic social events, while important, do not do the kind of job that is crucial for sustaining hope and motivation in the education task.

Skillfully Led Conversations Have a Structure

Stanfield suggests four crucial levels of questions for a skillfully led conversation (Stanfield, 1997, p. 18). These levels provide a flow that moves from very easy-to-answer questions about facts and observable data to very serious questions about decisions relative to those facts and data. The first, or objective, level of questions centers on recalled facts, data, observations, and information. Questions like: What did you notice? What struck you about _____? The second, or reflective, level of questions encourages feelings, relationships, and connections to emerge. Questions like: What were the characters feeling? What emotions were going on in the group then? Who did you identify with? The third, or interpretive, level of questions calls forth insights, reflections, or learning relative to the data, information, or item talked about. Questions like: Why is this important? What did you learn? What is the significance for your situation? Finally, the fourth, or decisional, level of questions moves the group to a decisional level. Questions like: What are our next steps? What are our options given this conversation? What would you say about our training when a colleague asks you about it?

To lead a conversation like this, it is necessary to think all of these questions through beforehand, paying attention to the flow and to the smoothness of the individual questions. It is always a challenge when leading to know when it is time to move to the next level. Being able to sense that will come with practice. As groups are not very practiced at experiencing this kind of conversation, it may take time for them to discover their own helpful ground rules. One of these is for individuals to steer away from dominating a group conversation. Short answers that are to the point are most helpful so that more in the group can participate. Another of these is the necessity to listen carefully to what a colleague is saying to get an accurate reading of what the colleague means. This requires temporarily suspending all tendencies to jump in or judge while the content from the colleague is digested carefully.

Table 4.1 pulls together these four levels with an image for each level and clue words as to what goes on in that level. Table 4.2 provides some sample questions that are appropriate for each level. A blank of this conversation planning form can be found in Template 13.

■ ACTIVITY SIXTEEN—INITIATE WHOLE-STAFF–GUIDED CONVERSATIONS

Description

It is possible for 10 to 60 people to participate in whole-staff–guided conversations. The leader poses questions one by one eliciting several responses to each question. These questions are constructed in such a way as to lead deeper and deeper into the conversation topic. As responses occur, even those who never say a word are participating by identifying with the responses. When these conversations are led well, the participants leave with a more profound connection, once again tied to their deep reasons for becoming teachers—they rejuvenate their commitment to what their vocation is all about.

Methodology

1. Remind oneself of the four crucial stages for guided conversations: Objective, Reflective, Interpretive, and Decisional.

Table 4.1   Leading Reflective Conversations—Discussion Method Flow

Objective		Facts Sensory date
Reflective		Emotions Feelings Associations
Interpretive		Values Meanings Purpose
Decisional		Resolves Options Next steps

SOURCE: Stanfield, R. B. (Ed.). (1997). *The art of focused conversation* (p. 23). Toronto, ON, Canada: The Canadian Institute of Cultural Affairs.

Table 4.2   Leading Reflective Conversations—Levels of Discussion/Conversation Questions

OPENING	What are the reasons for this discussion or conversation?
	Why has this meeting been called?
	What product is expected from this meeting?

OBJECTIVE	REFLECTIVE
What facts do we know about this?	What emotions did you observe?
What did you hear the speaker saying?	What are your own feelings?
What did you see?	What was your first response?
What do you remember from the presentation?	Where do you remember the whole group's reactions?
What pictures or images do you recall?	Where were you excited?
What words or phrases do you remember?	When did you feel upset or angry?
	Who did this remind you of?

INTERPRETIVE	DECISIONAL
Which are the most important ideas that came out in the presentation?	How would you tell someone about what has happened here?
What are the most critical implications from this video?	What are our next steps?
What are the crucial points we need to discuss to be able to make a decision on this?	What do you sense our consensus is so far?
Where do you sense the most struggles will be with this proposal?	What is the first thing you are going to do tomorrow?
Where do we have the most disagreement?	Who needs to be the first to hear about this?
	What change is needed in how we are operating at the present?
	What would you name this?

CLOSING	Where do we go from here?
	When do we meet again?
	Are our tasks clear for the next meeting?

2. Determine the focus, topic, or theme of the guided conversation.

3. Think through what the final question might be. This could be related to an action you are hoping people will take or a decision that you are hoping people will make.

4. From that, begin to build a question or two for the other stages.

5. Test the conversation question flow to see if you as the leader can answer the questions smoothly.

Examples

Table 4.3 suggests the flow of questions for a reflective conversation on the previous semester. Table 4.4 suggests the flow of questions for a reflective conversation on a classroom incident.

Metacognitive Insights

As people become more accustomed to such conversations, they automatically develop a consciousness about what is appropriate and what is not. People realize that such conversations are not times to jump in with disagreements or criticisms. Such conversations are times to listen. Such conversations are not times of lengthy responses. Short, concise responses enable more people to participate and share their wisdom about the topic being discussed. Such conversations are not times to try to dialogue with or ask questions to the conversation leader. As people develop this consciousness, the power of these conversations magnifies and transforms the group.

As a conversation leader, it takes practice to sense when the group is ready to move from one stage to the next. Some groups want to move on too quickly. Some groups signal they are ready to move by responses that lead nicely to the next stage.

ACTIVITY SEVENTEEN—USE ■
A GLOBAL EVENTS CONVERSATION

Description

A global events conversation is an excellent way to set the stage for a group's strategic planning or a group's discussion about what training needs to be emphasized in the coming year. This conversation begins by starting from the global and working down to the local. It concludes by naming some of the crucial trends. In this way, participants need to analyze all the material discussed and discover some common threads or themes.

Methodology

Objective

1. What has been happening around the world that has been influencing education (or any specific topic)?

Table 4.3   Conversation Flowchart—Reflective Conversation on the Previous Semester

OPENING	Before we do some planning for next semester, let's think some about our last semester.

OBJECTIVE	REFLECTIVE
What are some things that happened last semester? What are some things you will remember? Which students? Which class lessons especially?	What were some of your best moments? What pleased you in this last semester? Where were you surprised? When did you struggle?

INTERPRETIVE	DECISIONAL
As you have listened to our conversation, what are some of the themes that you have heard running through our responses? What journey have we made in our teaching this last semester? What have you learned? How are we as a school different?	What are some of your next steps relative to your students? What are you going to do next to increase your own teaching skills? What are our next steps as a whole school?

CLOSING	I'm really pleased with your good ideas for next semester.

Table 4.4   Conversation Flowchart—Reflective Conversation on a Classroom Incident

OPENING	Let's talk a bit about what happened this morning in class.

OBJECTIVE	REFLECTIVE
What actually happened? Who was involved? Who said what? What was said? Who said what when? What occurred just before this happened?	What feelings did people have? What did you feel? How do you feel now?

INTERPRETIVE	DECISIONAL
Why do you think this happened? What was really going on now that you have had a chance to think about it?	What might be some other ways for handling this? What are some alternative ways of dealing with these feelings? What needs to happen next?

CLOSING	Thank you for all of your participation and your good ideas.

2. What about happenings on a national level?

3. What has been going on regionally or locally that has impacted education?

Reflective

1. How has this affected you in your work?

2. What are concrete manifestations of this impact in your work?

Interpretive

1. What shifts have all of this generated in education?

2. In your reading or talking with others, what are some creative and positive directions or specific projects that have positively impacted the issues we are encountering in education?

Decisional

1. What are some of the broad positive trends going on that we need to take advantage of?

Example

Table 4.5 suggests the flow of questions as well as possible answers in a global events conversation.

Metacognitive Insights

A global events conversation helps people grasp the larger perspective. It enables participants in the conversation to see that many of the issues they struggle with are much larger than just a particular school's issues. Needless to say, the final question pushes the participants to realize there are positive trends and movements that can support what they believe needs to be happening in their schools.

■ ACTIVITY EIGHTEEN—EXPERIMENT WITH CLASSROOM CONVERSATIONS

Description

The classroom conversation discussed here follows the showing of a documentary film. Notice how it follows the flow of objective, reflective, interpretive, and decisional. Also note that everyone can participate in the initial, relatively easy objective-level questions.

Methodology

The conversation components that follow are adapted from Jo Nelson's book (2001) *The Art of Focused Conversation for Schools* (p. 71).

Table 4.5   Conversation Flowchart—Global Events Conversation

OPENING	Before we get down to planning, I'd like us to look at the larger picture for a few minutes.

OBJECTIVE	REFLECTIVE
What has been happening around the world that has been influencing education (or any specific topic)? *Technology, Iraq situation, War on Terror, migrations.* What about happenings on a national level? *NCLB, emphasis on accountability and high-stakes testing, school violence.* What has been going on regionally or locally that has impacted education? *Decreased state funding, drugs, scarcity in special ed, math, and science teachers.*	How has this affected you in your work? *Frustration, anger, depression.* What are concrete manifestations of this impact in your work? *Increased class size, pressure to increase test scores, fear of trying anything new in the classroom.*

INTERPRETIVE	DECISIONAL
What shifts has all of this generated in education? *More accountability, need for using more technology in the classroom, a more stressed environment in school.* In your reading or talking with others, what are some creative and positive directions or specific projects that have positively impacted the issues we are encountering in education? *Schools within a school, emphasis on literacy, creative scheduling.*	What are some of the broad positive trends going on that we need to take advantage of? *Globalization, technology, peer coaching, peer tutoring, peer mediation, business partnerships with individual schools.*

CLOSING	I believe our insights today will help us in our planning.

Objective

1. What visual pictures do you recall?

2. What words or phrases do you remember? Colors? Sounds?

3. What characters were featured in the video?

4. What happened first? Next?

Reflective

1. Where did the story sweep you in?

2. Where were you surprised or pleased?

3. Where were you upset or angry?

4. What other events or experiences did you think about?

Interpretive

1. What are some of the basic messages of the video?

2. What are some of the big issues or concerns revealed?

3. Which ones are you also concerned about?

Decisional

1. Individually, what concrete steps could you carry out to address this issue?

2. As a class, what could we do?

3. Who else do we need to get involved in this?

4. If some of these actions occur, what might be the result three years from now?

Example

Table 4.6 suggests the flow of questions for a conversation on a video about a historical event.

Metacognitive Insights

It is absolutely crucial not to shortchange the initial objective-level questions. To some, these questions may seem obvious. However, by laying a strong foundation of objective-level information, the leader makes sure that everyone is starting from the same place. Also, it is true that different people notice different things. So this objective level builds a common montage out of the individual viewings of the documentary.

Table 4.6   Conversation Flowchart—Conversation on a Video About a Historical Event

OPENING	Let's talk a bit about the video we have just seen.

OBJECTIVE	REFLECTIVE
What objects do you remember from the video? What words do you recall? What people do you remember? What scenes stick in your mind? In what order did these important scenes occur?	Who did you identify with? What parts of the video did you like? What surprised you? Angered you?

INTERPRETIVE	DECISIONAL
What did you learn? What were some of the crucial themes in this video? What issues in the video are still present today?	How could these issues be addressed today?

CLOSING	Thank you for your thought-filled responses.

■ ACTIVITY NINETEEN—DEMONSTRATE WINNING PARENT-TEACHER CONVERSATIONS

Description

The methodology for parent-teacher conversations can assist one in other one-to-one conversations. It can be used for teacher-to-teacher, teacher-to-student, and teacher-to-parent conversations, and so forth. This activity focuses on a conversation one might hold with a parent about a child who is having discipline problems.

Methodology

The conversation components that follow are adapted from Jo Nelson's book (2001) *The Art of Focused Conversation for Schools* (p. 177).

Objective

1. What have you noticed happening with your daughter in the last month or so?

2. What changes in behavior have you noticed recently?

3. What possible changes, if any, in the family situation might affect your daughter's behavior?

4. What other changes, if any, might be occurring in your daughter's life?

Reflective

1. What concerns you the most about your daughter's situation?

2. What are you relatively unconcerned about?

Interpretive

1. What do you think could be some reasons for this change in your daughter's behavior?

Decisional

1. What could be some ways we could work better with your daughter in school?

2. What could you do as her family for her?

3. The school and I are committed to _____.

4. What are ways we can be sure we are successful with this?

Example

Table 4.7 suggests the flow of questions as well as possible responses during a winning parent-teacher conversation.

Table 4.7   Conversation Flowchart—Winning Parent-Teacher Conversations

OPENING	Thank you for coming in today. I am so glad to have your daughter in my class.

OBJECTIVE	REFLECTIVE
What have you noticed happening with your daughter in the last month or so? *She suddenly seems moodier than usual.* What changes in behavior have you noticed recently? *She has been getting angry over the littlest things. It has been much harder to get her up in the morning.* What possible changes, if any, in the family situation might affect your daughter's behavior? *To be frank, my husband and I are considering a divorce right now.* What other changes, if any, might be occurring in your daughter's life? *More than likely, when the divorce goes through, my daughter and I will be moving to be closer to my parents.*	What concerns you the most about your daughter's situation? *She has been such a good student. I worry that a plunge in grades could have a long-lasting impact on her college and job possibilities.* What are you relatively unconcerned about? *Both my husband and I have assured her that we love her and care about her, and our relationship to her will not change.*

INTERPRETIVE	DECISIONAL
What do you think could be some reasons for this change in your daughter's behavior? *Clearly she is being hit by the possibility of a lot of changes and losses. Our home situation will change. She may not be able to see her friends here as regularly.*	What could be some ways we could work better with your daughter in school? *Perhaps someone here could talk with her openly about our family situation so that she knows she can talk freely about what is going on.* What could you do as her family for her? *Maybe I need to reconsider the move away from here. Also I need to pay more attention to her after school and encourage her in her studies.* The school and I are committed to making sure your daughter gets all the support she needs in this difficult time. What are ways we can be sure we are successful with this? *I would like to meet with you in five or six weeks to see if we are making progress here.*

CLOSING	Again, thank you for coming in today. Let's keep in touch.

Metacognitive Insights

Having a way to talk to parents in emotionally laden situations can do a great deal to boost the morale of teachers who often find this very emotionally draining for them. The temptation for the teacher is to talk too soon before giving the parent a chance to talk and defuse.

■ ACTIVITY TWENTY—RESPOND TO AN IRATE TEACHER

Description

One of the most trying experiences is dealing with someone who is extremely upset or even very angry. We may get intimidated, frustrated, or angry ourselves. None of the above internal responses is helpful in meeting these situations. Something like the following might be useful.

Methodology

Objective

1. Tell me what has happened.
2. Who were involved?
3. What was said?
4. When has this happened before?
5. How was it left?

Reflective

1. How did you react? How did you feel through this?
2. How were others feeling?
3. How are you feeling now?

Interpretive

1. What is your best sense of what is really going on here?
2. What is causing these people to react this way?

Decisional

1. How might this situation be improved or resolved?
2. Knowing all this now, how might you handle this differently next time?
3. How can I help?
4. Who else might be able to help both of us deal with this?

Example

Table 4.8 suggests the flow of questions as well as possible responses during a conversation responding to an irate teacher.

Table 4.8 Conversation Flowchart—Conversation Responding to an Irate Teacher

OPENING	Thank you for coming in. What occurred was very upsetting.

OBJECTIVE

Tell me what has happened. *I was in the middle of third period with my favorite class. Suddenly with no warning three of the guys are in a brawl on the floor.*

Who were involved? *Alphonso, Don, and Jethro.*

What was said? *Alphonso and Don accused Jethro of stealing Don's cell phone.*

When has this happened before? *Nothing like this has occurred before. I have noticed, however, that Jethro is very quiet and talks to very few people. Yet he is my top student.*

How was it left? *I asked each of then to write up what happened and how it could have been handled differently.*

REFLECTIVE

How did you react? How did you feel through this? *First I was in shock. Nothing like this has happened in my last eight years of teaching. Then I got really angry at such disregard for school and classroom guidelines.*

How were others feeling? *All three of the boys are angry at me now because I didn't side with any of them.*

How are you feeling now? *I am still very angry at them and also sad and depressed about the whole thing. Maybe there was something more I could have done.*

INTERPRETIVE

What is your best sense of what is really going on here? *I think Alphonso and Don are upset because Jethro is such a good student. They like to make fun of him. They tease him mercilessly.*

What is causing these people to react this way? *Alphonso and Don clearly don't like school. They are taking this out on Jethro who really loves school.*

DECISIONAL

How might this situation be improved or resolved? *I believe with a little more thought and attention, I can create projects and assignments that would get Alphonso and Don engaged in the class. They need to experience some success in school.*

Knowing all this now, how might you handle this differently next time? *First, I will be more alert for clues leading up to something like this. I have really ignored all their teasing of Jethro. I will make sure their teasing doesn't happen again. I know I feel so badly about how I handled this that I will be firm but not lose my cool in the classroom.*

How can I help? *Let's talk in two weeks and see how things are going.*

Who else might be able to help both of us deal with this? *I would like to talk to my classroom neighbor, Mr. Brown. I think he would be willing to help me if this occurred again. He has a third period class that is usually very well behaved. I could even trade places with him for a few minutes to allow him to help defuse the situation.*

CLOSING	Thank you for your thought-filled responses.

Metacognitive Insights

It is not necessary to use every one of the questions suggested for each level. This calls for the one asking the questions to be sensitive to the responses. If the leader feels that the level has been adequately explored, then the leader can move on to succeeding levels.

Note how the real burden of this situation is gently thrown back on the one who is angry or concerned. The conversation actually honors that person very directly by getting the input of that person in a structured, nonthreatening way. Also, note the valuable information the leader is getting about what is going on through this carefully constructed progression of questions.

■ ACTIVITY TWENTY-ONE—HOLD A "WHY I'M IN TEACHING" CONVERSATION

Description

Daily tasks often consume teachers' attention. Deadlines and difficult situations often dominate teachers' thinking. The purpose of the conversation discussed in this activity is to help a group remind itself why it got into teaching in the first place. It is very powerful and reaffirming not only to articulate to oneself what those reasons are but to hear fellow colleagues articulate why they got into teaching. Conversations like this one help to reinvigorate one's motivation and spirit.

Methodology

Objective

1. How many years have all of you been in education?

2. What have been some of the education roles or teaching levels you have been engaged in?

Reflective

1. What have been some of the high points of your careers?

2. What have been some of the low points of your careers?

Interpretive

1. What things have helped you stay in education?

2. When you were most discouraged, what did you tell yourself to keep teaching?

3. What motivated you to enter education in the first place?

4. What beliefs about teaching and education do you hold on to today?

Table 4.9   Conversation Flowchart—"Why I'm in Teaching" Conversation

OPENING	I'd like to have us talk a bit today about our journeys in teaching.

OBJECTIVE	REFLECTIVE
How many years have all of you been in education? *(Have someone record all the numbers of years and tally them up.)* What have been some of the education roles or teaching levels you have been engaged in? *Classroom teacher (elementary, middle, high school), special education teacher, physical education teacher, department head, assistant principal, etc.*	What have been some of the high points of your careers? *A year with a stellar sixth grade class. They worked hard and we clicked. The year I team taught. The year my students put on a play they wrote themselves for the whole school. The year our team won the championship. The year a rebellious student changed his whole attitude. Etc.* What have been some of the low points of your careers? *The year I had to flunk five of my students. Getting adjusted to a new principal. The year I was working on my Master's, teaching a new grade, and managing two young children of my own. Etc.*

INTERPRETIVE	DECISIONAL
What things have helped you stay in education? *I keep thinking of the teachers who made an impact on me. Teachers are sometimes the only consistency in a child's life.* When you were most discouraged, what did you tell yourself to keep teaching? *If I don't keep going on who will? My discouragement will pass. I will talk to my good colleague tomorrow—that will help me to feel better. Sometimes when discouraged, I read a thank you note a student sent me.* What motivated you to enter education in the first place? *I wanted to impact students the way some of my teachers impacted me. I believed that education could have a direct impact on the future. My father was a teacher. I saw how happy he was to be teaching.* What beliefs about teaching and education do you hold on to today? *I sincerely believe that it is possible to reach every student somehow. No two students are exactly alike in how they learn. We are losing a lot of students because we restrict our teaching to just one or two ways.*	What advice would you like to give someone just entering education today? *There is no better way to affect the future. No amount of money is worth more than when the light goes on in a child. You never know the full impact you are having on your students' lives. Occasionally a student returns to tell you. Those are precious moments.*

CLOSING	Thank you for your honest sharing today.

Decisional

1. What advice would you like to give someone just entering education today?

Example

Table 4.9 suggests the flow of questions as well as possible responses during a "Why I'm in Teaching" conversation.

Metacognitive Insight

This is a great conversation to hold at the beginning of the school year. Also, it is a helpful conversation to hold on the other side of a major setback or a frustrating schoolwide event. This conversation gives perspective on whatever the current mood or struggle is. It is a wonderful reminder of all the low points people have faced and survived.

5

Proclaiming Victorious Stories

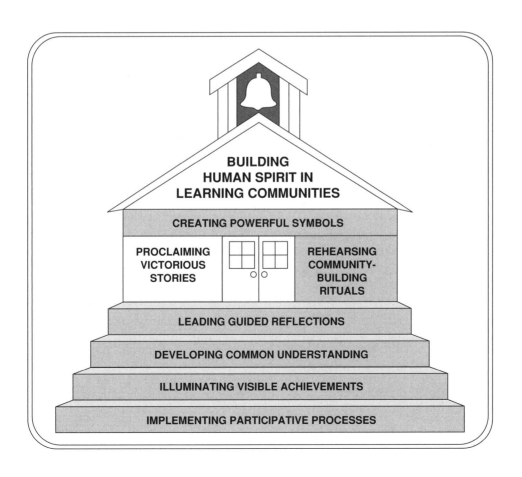

BUILDING HUMAN SPIRIT IN LEARNING COMMUNITIES

CREATING POWERFUL SYMBOLS

PROCLAIMING VICTORIOUS STORIES

REHEARSING COMMUNITY-BUILDING RITUALS

LEADING GUIDED REFLECTIONS

DEVELOPING COMMON UNDERSTANDING

ILLUMINATING VISIBLE ACHIEVEMENTS

IMPLEMENTING PARTICIPATIVE PROCESSES

Whatever the route to meeting objectives, the questions are the same: How do we recapture the magic and myth of education? How do we restore a mythology that enables teachers to believe in their importance and convince the public that schools are worthy of their confidence and support?

—Terrence E. Deal and Kent Peterson, 1999,
Shaping School Culture, p. 29

For several years, a high school district of four high schools had a group called the "Cadre." This group of teachers went through several days of training locally. In addition, individual teachers were often sent to extended training workshops outside of the district to hone their skills in various instructional areas. The intent of the Cadre was to implement staff development within the district. In other words, the self-story of the members of the Cadre was that they would lead workshops for their peers in various arenas of staff development. Because this was the story these teachers told themselves, many of them ended up leading very effective workshops for their peers.

More and more sources today are extolling the power of stories as key elements in building strong communities. We are reminded of the role stories played in the lives of the ancients. Stories were told and retold, passed down from generation to generation. In a day when analysis, logic, and data are increasing in importance, it is very possible to neglect this ancient wisdom.

■ STORIES HELP BUILD A CULTURE

"Historical lore and contemporary stories form the anchor and spirit of school culture" (Deal & Peterson, 1999, p. 58).

A school without victorious stories is a school without life. For a school culture to become more dynamic and engaging, stories need to be told and retold. Deal and Peterson seem to be suggesting that victorious stories are the lifeblood of a culture. "Culture is built on myth and stories" (DeForest, 1986, p. 221). When a story is told, both children and adults perk up, a different kind of listening occurs, and much more of the self gets invested. In addition, bonds among the people in the culture are strengthened and deepened as stories are told and retold (Deal & Peterson, 1999, p. 58).

In addition, the more real the relevant details, the more the story brings to life sights, sounds, smells, and tastes, the more impact the story has (Owen, 1987, p. 17). In this way a story comes to life and invites the listener into its power. In this way, the act that the story recounts becomes real before our eyes and ears. And the power of the original act gets felt all over again.

■ STORIES ENERGIZE A COMMUNITY

One of the reasons stories have such a profound effect on the school culture is because they energize a school community. In recounting past and present events, stories inspire connections and pride in a way that gives energy to the community (Deal & Peterson, 1999, p. 57). Stories reveal hidden truths that mere reports and highlights can't do. Stories have a way of universalizing a specific event so that many can identify with it and see its truth through events in their own lives.

> There is an advertisement on the radio for a high school military academy. In addition to extolling the benefits of their school program, they declare that every one of their graduates gets into college. That is the story that every student of that academy lives with. And, amazingly, it happens.

STORIES TRANSPORT US TO OTHER WORLDS BY ALLOWING US TO DREAM

Stories have a way of releasing us from the boundaries of the daily realities that over time restrict our hopes and dreams. In that way, we can say that stories transport us to other worlds (Bolman & Deal, 1995, p. 98). Stories have a way of allowing us to reconnect with our deep yearnings, our original decisions to be part of the education world. Consequently without stories we lose a pathway to those yearnings, and to those dreams.

More importantly for the school community, if there are no powerful stories, there are no community dreams. Needless to say, without dreams shared throughout the school community, the school stumbles and falters. Stories that foster dreams also encourage potential. In this way, then, stories have a unique gift in helping communities discern vision and direction.

STORIES CONNECT US TO LIFE'S SIGNIFICANCE AND MEANING

"We build significance through the use of many expressive and symbolic forms: rituals, ceremonies, icons, music, and stories" (Bolman & Deal, 1995, p. 110). Stories have the power to reveal significance and meaning to our lives. Stories help to transform the mundane reality of our everyday lives into a reality fraught with purpose and meaning. Without stories, all we see are struggling students, cramped schedules, overwhelming mandates, and growing accountability. Stories help us see value in the mundane and help us sustain hope in the future.

Students, teachers, administrators, and society are questioning whether education is working or whether education is still the key to the future. Stories can help us believe again in education's power (Deal & Peterson, 1999, p. 29). Stories that begin with the reality that people are experiencing and then reveal a victory through that reality can occasion that belief.

■ STORIES REVEAL MORAL PRINCIPLES

A story is an indirect way of communicating key principles. Because stories don't come out and overtly say, "You ought to do this" or "You really need to do that," they become much more palatable. In actuality the story leaves the implications up to the listener. In this way stories can become indirect moral anchors to guide the listeners. Many schools consider character education to be valuable these days. Stories can be prime vehicles for encouraging thought-provoking questions and decisions.

■ ACTIVITY TWENTY-TWO— CREATE A SCHOOL STORY

Description

This activity offers a relatively simple way to begin to write a motivating school story. By having people focus on the past, present, and future, people can provide the grist that will go in to the writing of a school story.

Methodology

1. Prepare three large pieces of chart paper to post strategically around the room. Label one of them *Past*, another *Present*, and the third *Future*.

2. Have people individually jot down words, phrases, or images that would fit each of the categories.

3. Beginning with the *Past*, have people share their brainstorming, writing all of this on the appropriate chart paper.

4. Do the same with the *Present* and *Future*.

5. When all three have been completed, divide the group into three teams.

6. Assign each team one of the areas: *Past*, *Present*, or *Future*.

7. Ask them to use the brainstormed data to create a paragraph or two on their assigned section.

8. Ask each team to create a graphic to go along with their assigned section.

9. When the teams have completed their work, have each team present what they have created.

10. Ask some processing questions after the reports, for example:
    a. What do you recall from the story?
    b. How do you feel about the story?
    c. What happened to this group as we heard this story?
    d. How would you like to use this story?

Example

The following is an example of what a story might look like.

Past

In the 1880s, immigrants from Europe settled our town. They were very committed and dedicated to education as well as to their work of farming. They located a teacher who was willing to teach the children. All of the children were in one classroom. The teacher was very well respected because in the summertime, the teacher worked in the fields alongside the farmers.

In the early 1900s, the school became so large that two elementary schools were built and a junior high school and high school were established. The schools in the district became known for the bands and the choirs. Mr. Jennings led the music program for 40 years, and music is still one of the hallmarks of this district.

In the late 1980s, the two elementary schools were consolidated and the high school was combined with neighboring high schools to become a regional high school. The new high school became known for its excellent math and science programs. Many graduates went on to institutions such as MIT and Stanford University.

Present

Today our schools look a lot different than they used to. There has been a large increase in minority students. Almost 40 percent of the student body is made up of Asian and Hispanic students, which has pushed our schools to increase the number of Asian and Hispanic teachers on the faculty. The challenge of a very diverse student population has been a struggle, but each year there seems to be more progress. Events like culture fairs have helped. Our music program integrates music from all over the world now. Our drama program does the same.

The biggest struggle today is getting adequate funding for the comprehensive school programs we have. Our teachers have worked hard to get grants to supplement state funding.

Future

We have just begun to integrate technology into the curriculum. As new computer labs have just been created in each school and computers are now in every classroom, we anticipate becoming known as the technology center in our region. We also see this as a way to reach out to the communities around us. Teachers and students have begun offering their time to teach their computer skills in adult education classes. A program of service learning, just begun last year, is transforming the attitude of the communities toward our schools. The possibility of more community support and more organizational support looks as if it will be a reality in our coming years.

Metacognitive Insights

This is a great activity for helping to integrate new staff people into the history and successes of a school. Depending on the purpose of this activity, support staff could also be involved in this writing. Bringing in community people, parents, and students to this activity could enhance the possibility of creating a story that will last for years.

■ ACTIVITY TWENTY-THREE— ENLIVEN STAFF MEETINGS

Description

In most workshops, teachers love sharing and talking with colleagues. They say they get very little time for real sharing in their daily schedules. Therefore one might assume that the regular staff meetings would help to fill some of that need. On the contrary, staff meetings often evolve into bureaucratic details and calendar announcements. Neither one of these is bad in itself—in fact, they are both necessary. My concern is sometimes that is all a staff meeting is. Consequently, teachers can leave the meeting feeling just as isolated and devoid of inspiration as before the meeting. The following is a proposed agenda and some dos and don'ts for staff meetings.

Methodology

> Agenda With Key Focus for the Meeting
>
> Icebreaker in Dyads or Triads
>
> Sharing Strategies That Are Working
>
> Focus Item: A Study or a Participatory Workshop
>
> Committee Reports and Announcements
>
> Closing

Template 14 provides an expanded form to use for planning a staff meeting.

Agenda With Key Focus for the Meeting

It is helpful, of course, to create an agenda for the meeting. Ideally this is done beforehand and sent to all of the participants. If not, displaying the agenda at the very beginning of the meeting can work. Even if it sounds similar to the last meeting, a written agenda helps people to feel there is a structure and a road map for the meeting. Highlighting the focus for the meeting gives people clarity on the one thing that the meeting is hoping to resolve.

Icebreaker in Dyads or Triads

I suggest two to three minutes of talking in dyads or triads, during which everyone has a chance to share with a partner or in groups of three something along the lines of a recent small victory, a new strategy being worked on, an exciting upcoming unit being prepared, and so forth. This helps to build cohesiveness in the group that will help whatever future decisions are required in the meeting.

Sharing Strategies That Are Working

Beyond the icebreaker, this part suggests a more detailed sharing from one or more teachers on a particular strategy that is working for them in the classroom. This could be as long as five minutes. It would be helpful to have it accompanied by some visual or, even better, a very short video of what is being shared. The purpose of this is to shore up the bottom line of a school—student learning and achievement. It also provides positive input for the teachers so they can leave the meeting feeling they have gotten something out of it that will help them in the classroom.

Focus Item: A Study or a Workshop

If the focus item is new material that needs to be covered, perhaps it could be covered with a study jigsaw method. Asking teams to take a chunk of the material, study it, and make a short presentation will be much more effective than the administrator talking through the material. Staff meetings can therefore model effective teaching.

If the focus item is input leading to a decision, a participatory workshop would be appropriate. Having the group respond with answers to a launch question or a key question will engage the participants. It is necessary for the leader to clarify all parameters or limitations ahead of time so that the brainstorming can generate realistic possibilities.

Committee Reports and Announcements

I have reserved short committee reports and announcements for the end of the meeting. If a committee report requires a decision, perhaps it belongs in the meeting focus. However, if it is merely informing the staff, this can be done toward the end along with brief announcements.

Closing

A short processing question is helpful to wrap things up. This could be one of the following questions: What have we accomplished today? What worked for us in terms of how we handled the meeting today? What is something you will take away from today's meeting?

Table 5.1 offers some simple dos and don'ts for a winning staff meeting.

Example

Table 5.2 shows an agenda for a staff meeting that follows the flow suggested in this activity.

Metacognitive Insights

Meetings held in formats like the one suggested in this activity can actually be meetings the staff looks forward to. When teachers feel they are genuinely participating in what is going on in the decision making of the school, it can boost their morale tremendously. This tells the teachers they are listened to and their experience counts.

Table 5.1   Dos and Don'ts

Dos	Don'ts
1. Encourage interaction, participation, and involvement.	1. Lecture the entire meeting.
2. Keep meetings focused.	2. Allow the meeting to go off into long, boring tangents.
3. Ask for only one big decision per meeting.	3. Expect several big decisions in one meeting.
4. Talk to people beforehand to get a reading of where the staff is.	4. Walk into a meeting with no idea where people are.
5. In times of crisis or high emotion, deal with the feelings directly. Nothing serious can happen until they are acknowledged and expressed.	5. Avoid emotions in a meeting.
6. Get staff input at every meeting.	6. Hold a meeting that is just input from the administrator with no chance for input from the staff.

Table 5.2   Meeting Agenda

Agenda With Key Focus for the Meeting
Key Question: Where can we put 10 new second graders?
Icebreaker in Dyads or Triads
With a partner, share something memorable about your week.
Sharing Strategies That Are Working
Five-minute report from Ms. Jackson on Problem Based Learning in her sixth grade class
Focus Item: A Study or a Participatory Workshop
Workshop on options for placing the 10 new fifth grade students, including staff shifts
Committee Reports and Announcements
Professional Development, Social and Community Relations Committees
Closing
Question: What have we accomplished today? Focus next week: A study on peer coaching

■ ACTIVITY TWENTY-FOUR— CELEBRATE VICTORIES QUARTERLY

Description

Marking victories quarterly keeps the focus on the victories, on the fact that the school is moving ahead and that victories are happening. Even if a particular teacher has had a rough quarter, a quarterly celebration can remind the teacher that victories have occurred throughout the whole school. There are two crucial pieces to a quarterly victory celebration. The first is that everyone needs to have an opportunity to name some of the victories. It is even more helpful if the victories can be written on cards or paper and posted on a wall. Once that has happened, it is vital to hold a conversation to reveal the wisdom learned from the victories and implications for the future out of these victories.

Methodology

1. Prepare ahead of time some visual tool like a star or a simple flower that can be used by people to write down their victories.

2. Think ahead of time whether there are some particular organizing themes that the victories could be placed around. These could be particular school emphases, themes, or strategies for the school year. Write these themes on visuals and place these on a wall. (A visual could be a star or balloon, etc.)

3. Have teacher teams brainstorm victories, projects, or accomplishments that have occurred in the particular time period.

4. Have these teams write the victories onto the visual, one victory per card.

5. Have the teams put their completed cards on the designated wall. If there are particular named emphases or themes, have them place the cards closest to the theme or strategy it best supports.

6. Once all the cards are up, gather people around the wall with the cards and hold a conversation, which may be initiated with some of the following questions:
   a. Which projects or accomplishments catch your attention?
   b. Which ones had you forgotten about?
   c. Which ones surprise you now?
   d. Which ones had the greatest effect on the students?
   e. Which ones had the greatest effect on the staff?
   f. Which ones had the greatest effect on the administration?
   g. Which ones had the greatest impact on parents and the community?
   h. Which ones were easier to complete?
   i. Which ones were difficult to complete?
   j. What messages are all these victories and accomplishments sending to us?
   k. What would be a good title for all of this?
   l. What next steps are being suggested for our school by all of this?

7. Ask for a volunteer to type all of this and distribute it to everyone present.

Example

Figure 5.2 illustrates the possible results of such a victory brainstorm.

Figure 5.2   Celebrate Victories

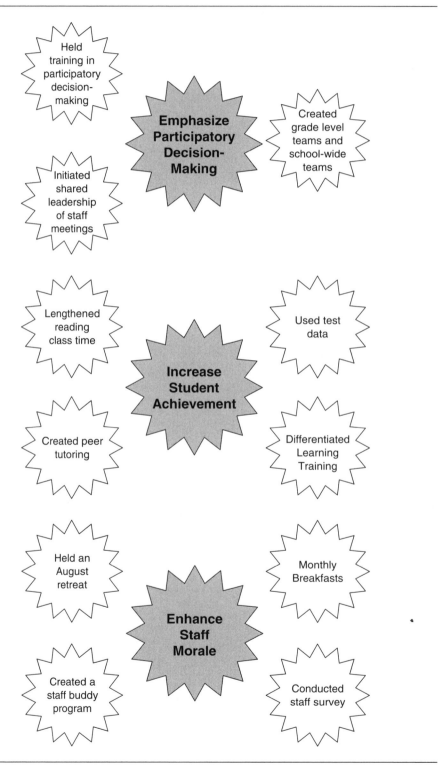

Metacognitive Insights

This very visual activity communicates the undeniability of the progress being made in the journey of the school. It can especially impact the doubters and the cynics of a staff. When done well, it encourages everyone to keep offering extra energy for the improvement of school morale. It is especially important to hold a reflective conversation after the workshop so people discern what's been learned and fully appreciate the impact of what's been shared.

ACTIVITY TWENTY-FIVE— OPEN THE SCHOOL DOORS   ■

Description

This activity is about getting the public into the school building. Given the many community populations in this country that are aging and the prevalence of households with no children in them, a huge percentage of this country's population has no connection with any school whatsoever. Given the rise of regional schools and magnet schools, today's schools are often divorced from the lives of local communities. Given the multicultural complexion of many of our communities, many parents and other community residents may feel intimidated by schools. Many schools are exploring innovative ways of building new connections with local communities and making the school facilities available to the public. It has to do with making a school a learning center for the whole community. It is time for the school to impact people of all ages in the community to fulfill its mission of educating the young. This is one way to get stories of victory spread throughout the community.

Methodology

1. Analyze data related to the needs and gifts of the community.

2. Come up with several ways to get people in the door that would serve the community.

3. Pick two or three to focus on, preferably ones that can begin with relatively little effort.

4. Pick ones that can also involve students in some capacity.

5. Work with the local community for feedback and help.

6. Publicize in various media.

7. Evaluate for effectiveness and response.

Example

Figure 5.3 illustrates a brainstorming procedure with the goal of getting people into the school.

Figure 5.3   Open the School Doors

	Felt	Real	
N E E D S	Taxes are too high. Community is aging. Young people have no values.	There is no connection between the school and the community. Young people are looked down upon.	WAYS TO GET PEOPLE IN THE DOOR Invite elders to lead workshops on their skills. Have students teach elders about e-mail.
	Community	**School**	
G I F T S	There are lots of elders with time on their hands. The community has skills needed in the school.	The school has a new regional facility. The school is interested in a service learning program.	

Some schools have begun evening and weekend classes for parents. Schools that have offered courses in computers for parents and the community have used some of their techno-savvy students to help teach them. One school opened its doors after the last class ended so that older people could do their walking inside in the halls, protected from inclement or cold weather. Other schools have discovered valuable community residents willing to come in and work with classes or talk to classes.

Metacognitive Insights

The fundamental goal is to build bridges between schools and the community. If there is ever to be more support for schools, more and more of the population needs to directly feel the benefit of their local school. In this way, opening the doors can open up a two-way street that dramatizes both the benefit of the school to the community and the benefit of the community to the school. In addition, some community people might be able to discern firsthand some of the needs the school has and advocate on behalf of the school.

■ ACTIVITY TWENTY-SIX—MARKET THE SCHOOL

Description

Many have considered marketing to be associated only with the world of business and commerce. These days, schools need to be aggressive in presenting a positive image of a school to the public. There are four big areas to consider in the realm of school marketing: constituencies, media, events, and networks. Developing strategies to impact all of these will dramatically improve the image of the school in the surrounding community and in the internal school community.

Methodology

1. Have a group from the staff brainstorm elements of each of the four areas: constituencies, media, events, and networks. If the brainstorm does not seem complete, more can always be added later.

2. Have all the brainstorming posted visually on a front wall. The list could be on cards or on pieces of paper.

3. Divide the group into four parts, one for each area.

4. Ask each group to study its particular list. Have them add any more items that come to their attention as they study the list.

5. After studying the list, ask each group to come up with some actions that would help foster support or awareness of their school in their particular area.

6. The more each group can list actions that they themselves will do and carry out the better. It is not too helpful for them to make a list of lots of things for someone else to do.

7. Have each group lay out their actions, stating what the actions are, when they will be done, who will do them.

8. Hold a short conversation with questions like these:
   a. What have we accomplished?
   b. What insights have occurred to you as you worked on this?
   c. What different place will you be in several months from now if most of this happens?

Example

Table 5.3 offers the possible results of a brainstorming session in the four areas of constituencies, media, events, and networks.

Table 5.3   Sample Brainstorm

Constituencies	Media	Events	Networks
Students	TV	Job fair	Nearby schools
Parents	Radio	Culture fair	Colleges and universities
Community	City newspaper	Family reading night	Chambers of commerce
Teachers	Local newspaper	School Open House	Local businesses
Administrators	Internet	School play	Service clubs
Support staff		School music	Churches
School Board		program	Social agencies
Community			
Leaders			
County and state			
Politicians			

Metacognitive Insights

Marketing is really about telling the stories of the great things going on in a school. The overt purpose is to beam positive images of the school to the community and to the parents. In addition, this marketing will help to transform the school community as staff communicates to others what positive things are going on in the school.

■ ACTIVITY TWENTY-SEVEN— BUILD SUPPORTIVE NETWORKS

Description

For too long the educational community has existed separate from the community itself. The growth of regional schools has by necessity taken the school out of smaller communities, thus distancing schools from many community constituents. As the population ages, it becomes harder for much of the public to experience a relationship to a school. This is why it is becoming so important for a school to create connections and build supportive networks. It is also crucial for schools to understand that even as needy as a school may feel it is, the benefits of network connections go both ways.

Methodology

1. Begin by having the group brainstorm organizations, companies, and institutions that are in the area.

2. Have people brainstorm on one color of 5×8 card the organizations, companies, institutions, and networks to which the school is currently connected.

3. On a different color of card, have the group brainstorm organizations, companies, businesses, and institutions they would like the school to be related to in some way.

4. Post the cards around some image or picture of the school.

5. Brainstorm ways the school can increase its network in the coming six months to a year.

6. Make sure that there is a specific plan with concrete action steps, when the steps will be completed, and who will be responsible for each step.

7. Pick two or three of the suggested networks the school is not yet connected to.

8. Have people brainstorm two things for each organization, company, or network.
   a. How would the school benefit from such a connection?
   b. How would the organization, company, or network benefit from a closer connection to the school?

9. After completing two or three of these, ask the group what they are discovering.

10. Make sure everything is typed up and documented for future meetings.

Example

Table 5.4 shows a brainstorming of current networks and possible networks. Table 5.5 represents a detailed action plan for involving community senior citizens. Note the three columns of the specific task, who is responsible for accomplishing the task, and the deadline by which the task needs to be completed. Table 5 .6 summarizes a brainstorming on the benefits to

Table 5.4   Networking Brainstorm

Current Networks		Possible Networks
PTA District schools Retired teachers Parents School Board Support staff		Chamber of Commerce Local college Rotary Media Major employers Community senior citizens Political leaders Museums

Table 5.5   Action Plan for Involving Community Senior Citizens

Action	Responsibility	Completion Date
Call the Senior Citizens Center.	Mr. Rose	October 1
Ask to make a presentation on reader volunteers.	Mr. Rose	October 1
Prepare a sign-up chart.	Mr. Samuels	October 15
Include in the presentation a senior citizen and a young student, modeling what the interaction might look like.	Ms. Valdez	October 20
Plan a Welcoming Tea for the volunteers who sign up.	Mr. Wilson and Ms. Rosario	October 20
Hold the Welcoming Tea.	Planning Committee	October 30
Make sure each volunteer is connected to one teacher.	Mr. Rose and Ms. Valdez	October 30
Schedule periodic check-ins with the volunteer to see how it's going.	All the teachers	Once a month until June

Table 5.6   Network Connecting Benefits

Benefits to the School	Benefits to the Senior Citizens
More adult contact for the students.	Connection to the younger generation.
Assistance on literacy.	Feeling a significant use of their time.
Connection to the elder generation.	Something to look forward to.
Senior citizens see the school needs.	A chance to impart some of their experiences.

the school of involving the senior citizens and on the benefits to the senior citizens of becoming involved in the life of the school.

Metacognitive Insights

I suspect that most school staff members can't imagine how a network connection with their school would provide a benefit to the participating network. This activity both expands people's grasp of how many networks are available, as well as how such connections can benefit the network. Building human spirit and uplifting the morale of a school will be greatly enhanced by network connections.

■ ACTIVITY TWENTY-EIGHT— GET THE POLS IN THE DOOR

Description

It is common to hear educators talk about how little people in government positions really understand about life in a school. We can't fault people for retaining the image of school they developed as they were growing up and attending school. Of course, teachers know today how much life has changed in our schools. This calls for schools to create ways to get people in political office inside the school buildings to get a taste of what really goes on.

Methodology

The key to getting people in political office in the door is to create events that will interest them or appeal to them as great photo opportunities.

1. First, it is crucial to get the whole school staff or a good number of them behind the idea of inviting some politicians into the school. This won't work well if only a few people are behind it.

2. Brainstorm some possible events that could draw a politician. These could be schoolwide events, celebrations, or festivities. However, it is crucial to build into the flow some way for the politician to visit a classroom or two or to have conversations with some of the teachers. The reason for this is to help a politician grasp the realities of school life and school challenges.

3. Decide on one or two events.

4. Brainstorm which other networks or individuals in the community would support this event and support a politician visiting the school.

5. Create a task force.

6. Build a detailed action plan for all of the steps necessary to pull off this event. Perhaps smaller teams will need to be created to divide up the work.

7. Be sure to pay attention to getting plenty of media, lots of community representation, and parent involvement.

Example

Possible Events

Schoolwide festivals

High school level debates

Election-theme projects to coincide with election time

Asking a political person to judge a contest

Inviting a political person to come and talk about what they have done for the local community or state

A school award for the political person

Metacognitive Insights

Notice how everyone benefits in this activity. The school gets a chance to show off as well as a chance to communicate the realities of school life to someone who can have influence over state policies. The politician benefits because he or she is seen as someone concerned about schools. The community will benefit with good publicity. Stories are shared and spread.

6

Rehearsing Community-Building Rituals

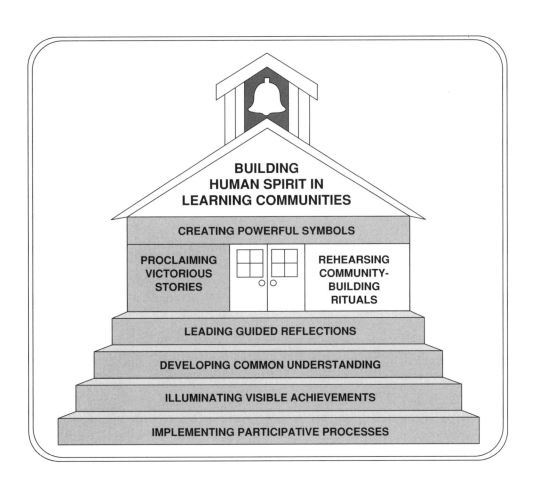

BUILDING
HUMAN SPIRIT IN
LEARNING COMMUNITIES

CREATING POWERFUL SYMBOLS

PROCLAIMING
VICTORIOUS
STORIES

REHEARSING
COMMUNITY-
BUILDING
RITUALS

LEADING GUIDED REFLECTIONS

DEVELOPING COMMON UNDERSTANDING

ILLUMINATING VISIBLE ACHIEVEMENTS

IMPLEMENTING PARTICIPATIVE PROCESSES

. . . our daily or weekly rituals provide a welcome chance to reflect and connect. We renew ourselves, bond with others, and experience life's deeper meaning in our everyday liturgy.

—Terrence E. Deal and Kent Peterson,
1999, *Shaping School Culture*, p. 31

For many summers, a group of teachers from several schools who participated in a networking program (which encouraged teaching that inspired higher-order thinking by the students) met for a week of further training. The week began with a welcoming dinner on Sunday evening. By Thursday evening, everyone had had four intensive days of workshops. To close the week, there was a special dinner together Thursday evening, followed by skits—each school represented at the workshop created its own skit. Some skits were outrageously humorous; others were clever reminders of things taught that week; they all became a magnificent reminder of the intensity and spirit the participants derived from their experience together. Creativity went wild. These skits provided a way to stamp the week forever into people's minds and hearts.

Toward the end of a long workshop, it is often possible to do a five-minute culminating activity. Each team of five or six people spends five minutes creating a pantomime, a rap, a poem, a song, a poster, or a TV ad promoting the particular subject of the workshop. Five minutes might seem very short, but it is amazing to discover the creative thinking that is released during those five minutes. By rehearsing the key points of the workshop, often in a humorous way, the message of the workshop gets stamped into memory in a very different way than during the workshop.

Rituals are simple. They might be words. They might be actions. They point to something meaningful and significant. In this way they broadcast meaning and significance to whatever is going on. For Owen, "Ritual is simply putting the words of myth into form, motion, and music" (Owen, 1997, p. 12). In other words, ritual is a way of expressing the deep message and intent of the story. When the stories are real, meaningful, and powerful, so will the rituals be that arise out of those stories. When the stories are well-known, then the relatively short ritual can quickly bring one back into the transforming power and energy of the story.

The students of a middle school all participated in a simple ritual at the beginning of each school day. After reciting the Pledge of Allegiance (another ritual), each student recited something like this: "I come ready and prepared for school. I bring my pencil so that I can work. I will have a great future."

Kriete in an article from *Educational Leadership* describes how she and other teachers begin their day with their students. She begins by having students greet the students next to them. The form of the greeting might change each day. A few students are then given an opportunity to share anything they want to mention. Afterward, a student who has shared invites comments or questions. The teacher then leads an activity for the whole group to build cohesion and community. Finally, the class looks at what will be happening for the rest of the day. Kriete (2003, pp. 68–70) believes this 30 minute "ritual" helps create the sense of inclusion, caring, and trust crucial for successful school work.

Rituals can be as simple as morning programs such as described by Kriete or they can be elaborate ceremonies. Graduations, recognition assemblies, special whole-school activity days are all examples of more elaborate ceremonies. They can all have the potential of rituals outlined in this chapter.

RITUALS INFUSE TIME WITH MEANING   ■

Well-thought-out rituals have a way of transforming the daily and the mundane into something special. "When ritual and ceremony are authentic and attuned, they fire the imagination, evoke insight, and touch the heart" (Bolman & Deal, 1995, p. 111). When the heart is touched, motivation grows; morale builds; and pride deepens.

Whether it is a one-minute daily opening or an extended ceremony like a graduation, the ritual provides an opportunity for reflection, a chance to remember once again what your life is about, whether you are a student, teacher, or administrator. School life provides a multitude of events that can become meaningful rituals: Opening day for the school year, homecoming when alumni are gathered and recognized, holiday celebrations, recognition ceremonies, celebrations of diversity, and of course year-end celebrations like graduations. All of these rituals strengthen the bonds among the school community and help students, teachers, and administrators weather the tremendous pressures each faces. "We are connected with an energy force beyond ourselves" (DeForest, 1986, p. 231).

A number of special programs have been created over the last couple of decades to help youth who have gotten into various kinds of trouble. Some of these programs have been developed as places of last resort for these youth. Many of them have incorporated a number of crucial rituals. Some have borrowed rituals from the American Indian tradition, such as the use of the four compass directions to symbolize important concepts. Certain stages of the journey through this program are marked with rituals to mark their significance. Participation in these rituals may come off labored and forced in the beginning. Gradually, however, they become highly important and meaningful to these youth.

RITUALS OF CELEBRATION   ■
AND CEREMONY MARK TRANSITIONS

Transitions become powerful when marked with celebration or ceremony. It is one thing to let a beloved principal walk out the door. It is quite another thing to create a ceremony where her gifts and her person are honored. This does something for the person honored, of course. But more important, it helps to smooth the difficult letting go that each staff person faces.

It is one thing for a student to take home a stellar report card. It is quite a different thing for that student to be part of an assembly honoring many students for their schoolwork. When done well, this fosters the kind of pride in learning that enables students to continue to be lifelong learners.

It is one thing for a teacher to acknowledge positively a student's ethnic heritage. It is quite another thing for an entire school to hold a diversity or multicultural fair where many ethnic groups are celebrated and honored. This kind of ceremony builds bonds and deepens pride in a unique way. "Celebrations weave our hearts and souls into a shared destiny" (Bolman & Deal, 1995, p. 96). In some magical way, ceremonies and celebrations that are well carried out build meaning and significance into the life of a group, organization, or community. Stated more bluntly, without ceremony and celebration, something terrible is missing in transitions; they feel unfinished or incomplete (Bolman & Deal, 1995, p. 110).

I can't emphasize enough that such ceremonies and celebrations do not just happen automatically. Just because people gather, it doesn't mean the experience will be meaningful or significant. "Such events become caring celebrations when they are planned beforehand and have a basic structure or program" (Stanfield, 2000, p. 24).

A consultant was called to work with teachers of a small school on an American Indian Reservation. The two-day workshop went smoothly. The group and the consultant seemed to bond well and the participants talked about how much they had learned in the workshop. As the end approached, it was clearly a time to celebrate the hard work. Each team was given the task of creating some way to celebrate the workshop in two or three minutes. One team had individuals write notes to others stating what they appreciated about their participation. Another team had the whole group go outside and look at the sky as a way to celebrate the "sky's-the-limit" feeling after their workshop. Another team created a little song to sing to everyone. Although this happened 10 years ago, the consultant recalls vividly the power of those moments of celebration. She suspects that many of the participants do too.

■ MEANINGFUL RITUALS FOSTER LEARNING

Initially, it may seem like a huge stretch to make a connection between rituals and ceremony and significant learning. Yet we have acknowledged that meaningful rituals and ceremonies can have a powerful effect on the sense of community and cohesion. The school community's focus is education—teaching and learning. Whatever binds the community together more strongly can only have a positive impact on the community's focus. Learning is increased "by strong traditions, frequent ritual, and poignant ceremonies" (Deal & Peterson, 1999, p. 32).

One way to understand this is to think about the security and predictability that ritual and ceremony provides both teachers and students. By creating an atmosphere that is at least somewhat predictable, anxieties are lowered and more learning is possible.

RITUALS CAN CONVEY DEEPER ■ VALUES AND PURPOSES

Meaningful rituals and ceremonies provide a very indirect way to convey and support community core values and beliefs. It doesn't always work to state outright "This is what you ought to value or believe." Yet when hidden and incorporated into meaningful rituals and ceremonies, they can enter into minds and hearts that might otherwise be closed. Ritual has the potential of allowing people to touch common values and beliefs (Deal & Peterson, 1999, p. 31).

In fact this means that when rituals and ceremonies are planned, a great deal of thought needs to go into exactly what is trying to be communicated during the ritual and ceremony. A slight turn of the dial can add a depth of meaning that can make all the difference between a routine and a ceremony.

This means paying attention to any symbols used, any stories referred to, the particular way a person or people will be recognized, the specific words to be used, who is to attend and where they will sit, and so forth (Deal & Peterson, 1999, p. 40).

DeForest (1986, p. 216) uses the phrase "conscious celebrations." Again, this points to the necessity to construct a ritual or ceremony very carefully so that it will convey precisely what is needed and wanted. A conscious celebration can be a high point, uplifting the spirit of all who participate.

ACTIVITY TWENTY-NINE— ENHANCE SCHOOL SPIRIT WITH ■ SHORT, RELEVANT SCHOOL RITUALS

Description

Rituals can be spoken. Rituals can be regularly recurring events. Rituals can be whole-school or individual classroom procedures. Rituals, when done with focus and attentiveness, can tap intuitive ways of connecting people together.

Methodology

1. Discern the hallmarks or unique qualities of the school or class.

2. Write them on chart paper so that all can see them.

3. Determine whether a verbal ritual or another kind of ritual is most appropriate.

4. Divide the group into teams to come up with possible ritual suggestions.

5. Have the groups share the suggestions.

6. Either modify the suggestions to incorporate the gifts of more than one or choose the one that best fits the group's intents.

7. Practice these rituals so that they become second nature.

8. Change when the rituals appear to have lost their power.

Example

As mentioned previously, the students of a middle school had a daily ritual of stating something like: *"I come to school ready and prepared to learn. I bring my books and pencils. Learning will help guide me to a brighter future."*
Another ritual might go like this:

The teacher: *"Who are you?"*

The students: *"We are citizens of tomorrow."*

The teacher: *"What are we about?"*

The students: *"We are about unlocking the secrets of our universe."*

The teacher: *"Why do we do this?"*

The students: *"So that we can build caring communities."*

A very simple ritual related to classroom management is the raised hand of a teacher followed by all the students raising their hands as a signal to quiet down and focus forward. This simple ritual can take the place of a raised voice and is extremely useful after cooperative teams have been working in groups for a length of time.

Metacognitive Insights

The power of rituals lies both in their ability to create cohesion and in their ability to remind one of deeper realities. In the franticness of contemporary life, in the hurried schedules of everyone in school communities, it is easier to forget the role of education and learning in creating meaningful culture. Rituals provide a moment of reflection, a moment of connecting with the deeper purposes of education.

■ ACTIVITY THIRTY—CAPITALIZE ON EXCITING SCHOOLWIDE EVENTS

Description

Once or twice a year schoolwide events can become powerful unifiers. Such events can break down age barriers, grade-level barriers, and, when done well, dramatically increase the spirit and mood of everyone in the school community. These can also be opportunities to put the school in the public spotlight in a very positive way. Schoolwide events can be very appealing for the media to feature.

Methodology

1. Encourage the participation of several school community personnel. The more people who are a part of the planning, the better the chance of having a stellar schoolwide event.

2. Have people define what their criteria will be for choosing the exact nature of the event (ability to draw interest, potential for creativity, educational value for all levels of students, etc.).

3. When the specific event has been chosen, consider aspects of planning such as
   a. *Space*—Where will this take place? How can the location be made welcoming and have an impact? What décor will be helpful? What will seating arrangements or table arrangements look like?
   b. *Time*—When is the best time of the year for this? How long an event (several hours, one day, two days, one week) will it be? What time of day is best for this event? How can the event flow smoothly and in a way to keep interest heightened?
   c. *Eventfulness*—What occurrences will keep the mood and interest high? How can students be involved in a way to promote parent involvement? What will make this a memorable event?
   d. *Product*—What are we hoping to have happen as a result of this event? What might we offer (even something simple) for the attendees to take home?
   e. *Style*—What kind of mood are we interested in projecting? What can we do to enhance that mood? How can we make sure that everyone who attends is comfortable and has a good experience?

Figure 6.2 illustrates the elements of planning for a successful schoolwide event.

Example

The following are some events that could become very successful:

Career Night

Multicultural Week

Student Portfolio Night

Historical Reenactment

Metacognitive Reflection

It is often easier to get support and energy for an event that is planned for, carried out, and then is over. People who won't be a part of a permanent committee will often be willing to support something they can see the end of. With the time that will necessarily be spent on this, it most certainly needs to be tied in some way to curriculum so that the students will gain academic information or usable skills through preparation and participation in this event.

Figure 6.2   Successful Schoolwide Event Elements

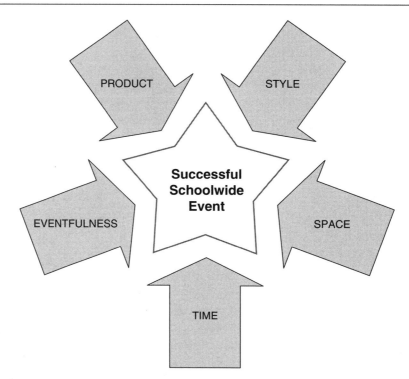

SOURCE: Adapted from Spencer, L. (1989). *Winning through participation*, pp. 81–82. Dubuque, IA: Kendall/Hunt.

■ ACTIVITY THIRTY-ONE—ALLOW TEAM SLOGANS TO COME ALIVE

Description

The power of a slogan is its ability to state succinctly, oftentimes in a catchy manner, the core of a message. This slogan is usually repeated over and over again. Gradually it becomes a natural part of people's consciousness. Needless to say, the advertising world has been on to this for decades. "Good to the last drop and that drop's good too." "Fly the friendly skies of United." "We try harder." And it's not just advertising: for example, "faster than a speeding bullet." These slogans conjure up very specific images and are powerful reminders. It is possible for school teams to create such symbols.

Methodology

1. Brainstorm the values that might be helpful to communicate in a slogan.

2. Choose two or three of these values to be the primary focus.

3. Divide people into groups of two or three.

4. Ask each group to create a simple slogan in five minutes.

5. At the end of five minutes, ask each group to share what they have even if it is only one word or a beginning phrase.

6. List them on chart paper.

7. Discern some connections or commonalities.

8. Build the slogan.

9. Go back and check to see if it communicates the values focused on in step 1.

Example

A group of high school math teachers want to create a slogan together. They meet to brainstorm such key values as: math is vital to the 21st century; math is the entry to a great future; math is crucial to this age of technology; math is the ticket to the future. Then they focus on the importance of math to the futures of their students. Working in teams of two or three they come up with a few possibilities: Math—passport to an exciting future; Math—the key to unlocking future power; Math multiplies your possibilities. Working together, the teams twist things around a bit and end up with: *Math adds to your power and multiplies your skills.* Note how this slogan translates math into a clear benefit for both the teachers and the students.

Metacognitive Reflection

The key to a slogan's power is that it is easy to recall. For the group of teachers in our example, whenever they recite the slogan they will unconsciously recall the conversations that led up to its creation—more than just the slogan is retained. Allowing teams of students to create a slogan for their own cooperative groups can be a way both to remind the students of their educational focus as well as provide a bonding reinforcement.

ACTIVITY THIRTY-TWO—DEMONSTRATE THE POWER OF SERVICE LEARNING

Description

Service learning involves students participating in a project of service to the community or school. Service learning is most powerful when it is connected to a significant aspect of the academic curriculum. Although the impact will obviously be felt in the community and may do a lot to improve the community's image of the students, the impact will also be felt within the lives of the students who participate. Teachers have talked to me about the changes they have seen in student attitudes because they have participated in a well-planned and well-carried out service learning project (Fogarty, 1997, *Problem-Based Learning and Other Curriculum Models*, p. 103).

The critical elements of the service learning experience include the following:

1. Selecting the need for service
2. Finding a community partner
3. Aligning the service experience with educational goals
4. Managing the project or program
5. Fostering reflective student learning throughout the process

Methodology

1. Select the need for service.
   a. Have the class brainstorm possible projects they would be interested in.
   b. Have the class brainstorm criteria that would be appropriate in choosing which project to do.
   c. A matrix might help them see visually which project embodies the most criteria.

2. Find a community partner.
   a. Have the class brainstorm possible community partners. (The teacher may need to do some research to augment the class's knowledge.)
   b. Have the class choose two or three of the most likely partners.
   c. Ask for volunteers to contact representatives to see if there is interest in becoming a partner.
   d. Have the volunteers report back.
   e. Finalize a community partner.

3. Align the service experience with educational goals.
   a. It is the teacher's job to do the aligning. Service learning that is not connected with standards or educational goals may waste valuable teaching time.
   b. The teacher needs to find ways to make the class clear about the standards or goals to be met during the service learning project.

4. Manage the project or program.
   a. Again, this falls largely on the teacher. It is crucial to delineate a realistic project that can be accomplished within the defined time frame.
   b. Cooperative learning group structures can definitely assist the teacher in managing this project.
   c. The teacher needs to discern how to make sure each student has achieved educational goals.

5. Foster reflective student learning throughout the process.
   a. In addition to the content of the educational goals, the teacher needs to create methods to help engage student reflection.
   b. Weekly journals, sentence stems, summary papers are all possible ways to do this.
   c. It is crucial to note that both the educational goals and the personal insights gathered are important for the growth of the whole student.

Example

A school in a large city was concerned about the trash around a nearby river. Many students passed by it as they walked to school. In doing some research, they discovered that there was a statewide organization whose concern was the health of the state's rivers. Working with them, they targeted an area near the school on which to concentrate their efforts. The students worked once a week during their social studies class period. With assistance from a volunteer from the statewide organization, they were able to make a huge difference in the appearance of that river site. Meanwhile the social studies teacher was able to link their work with their science class, which was studying the environment, and also their health class, which was studying the spread of communicable diseases. The teacher, in conversation with the volunteer, knew exactly how much they wanted to accomplish. She broke the task down into eight segments to be completed during the eight weeks early fall. She created several teams and named team leaders who made sure everyone in their particular class was involved. Each team wrote up a report at the end of each session detailing what they were able to accomplish. At the end of the eight weeks, she asked the students to comment on what they had discovered during their project. Many of the students detailed specifically what they had learned relative to their environmental and health curricula. Others commented on how good it felt when community people stopped by and thanked them for their hard work. Others noted with pride the small sign that was erected mentioning the work of their class. Others wrote about how proud their parents were of their efforts.

Metacognitive Reflection

A project such as the one described in this activity can be a tremendous opportunity to boost the morale of both student and teacher. It is also a concrete way to dramatize that school learning can have an impact outside of the walls of the school. Furthermore, the contact that may result with the community partners and other adults observing the project can expand the students' positive adult relationships.

ACTIVITY THIRTY-THREE—RECOGNIZE STUDENT AND TEACHER PERFORMANCE ■

Description

Recognition is not expensive, yet it goes a long way in boosting morale in the life of a school. Recognition is also a way to emphasize the values held high by a school, and academic recognition is the bottom line. However, recognition can also be given for improvement, creativity, team work, and so forth. Recognition can also go to teachers. Recognition can go to whole classes. How recognition happens is as important as the recognition itself. A cut-and-dry, "just because it is always done this way" recognition soon becomes old hat and loses meaning. The trick is blending elements we have already been talking about into the recognition: elements such as story, drama, and song.

Methodology

1. Involve a cross-section in the planning group. Perhaps students can be included.

2. Have the group decide what needs to be recognized and why.

3. Encourage inclusiveness in student recognition: academics, arts, physical education, team building, creativity, and so forth.

4. Encourage teacher recognition: a teacher who pulled off a remarkable unit, a teacher who put a lot of time into a drama production, a teacher who has been teaching at the school for a long time, a teacher whose class score has improved a great deal, and so forth.

5. Generate a theme for the recognition.

6. Unleash the creativity to decide what the recognition will look like as well as how the event will flow. Consider parent involvement in the planning.

7. This event does not need to be long. A 30-minute lively, creative event will go much further than an hour event that is poorly planned.

Example

There are many ways to hold such an event:

An assembly.

A recognition breakfast before school.

An evening meal.

A ceremony held over the intercom.

The ones recognized have lunch together.

The ones recognized go on a field trip together.

The ones recognized go to a sporting event together.

Metacognitive Reflection

Such a recognition event with a dynamic, lively flow will go far in building cohesion and morale in the life of a school. If such events happened quarterly, the impact would soon become visible to all. The trick is to keep such recognition events changing so that they don't become old hat.

7

Creating Powerful Symbols

Recent brain research and the writings of such people as Carl Jung and Jean Houston have raised awareness of the world of symbols. Celebrations in the past have been rich in the use of symbols, from the Japanese Noh plays to the Greek Festivals of Dionysius. In today's world symbols can offer the culminating image that bonds the meaning of a ritual and enables the celebration to live beyond its temporary existence.

—Cathy DeForest, 1986, "The Art of Conscious Celebration:
A New Concept for Today's Leaders," in John
Adams (ed.), *Transforming Leadership*, p. 220

W e are all familiar with symbols. The advertising world is adept at creating them. There is the car advertisement with "zoom, zoom." Or the coffee cup dripping the last drop of coffee—"And that drop's good too." The flag of a nation often becomes a very powerful symbol. Many people around the world are now familiar with "9/11." Many families have their own family crests. Schools have adopted mascots or other visual symbols for their schools. Most schools have school colors. All of these tap the power of symbols. Some schools have found it helpful to symbolize student unity by having all the students wear a uniform. Teachers in Japan, even in cold winters that make classrooms quite cold, would never wear an overcoat so that they present proper dress to their students at all times.

A principal once mentioned that he spends 50 percent of the school day wandering around the school talking to teachers and students just to keep tabs on all that is going on. A high school principal always appeared in the hallways during class changing time to greet both the teachers and the students. Another principal told me she spent at least 80 percent of her school day visiting classrooms, watching the teaching going on. These principals were using their symbolic power to carry out what they decided was important in leading their schools.

Throughout history visual symbols have drawn people together and helped people experience connections with deeper values and purposes. When these symbols are connected to important aspects of people's lives and experiences, they have a way of resonating deep within whenever they are viewed. Because of this it is important to consider symbols whenever one's intent is to build morale and spirit in a school.

■ SYMBOLS RECONNECT PEOPLE WITH THEIR COMMITMENT AND BELIEFS

If we are out to bring life into the institution of school, then attention needs to be paid to what instills that life. Deep beliefs, meaningfulness, and hope call forth engagement in life. Symbols are one of the sources of commitment and hope. "Every school or classroom as does every human group, creates symbols to cultivate commitment, hope, and loyalty" (Bolman & Deal, 2002, p. 4). Symbols point to the invisible cultural values and beliefs underlying the life of any community (Deal & Peterson, 1999, p. 60). A symbol's power increases when it is linked to the regular use of stories and rituals.

SYMBOLS SHOW UP IN MANY WAYS   ■

Symbols are everywhere. In the life of a school the potential for powerful symbols is even more possible than in many other places. As this section suggests, there is nothing strange or new about symbols. What may be given new consideration is what a crucial role symbols play in the life of a learning community.

I would suggest there are at least five major ways symbols can show up in the life of schools. Symbols can

1. Project an *inviting style*

2. Celebrate a *meaningful heritage*

3. Enhance *school pride*

4. Herald *academic excellence*

5. Create an *empowered staff*

Table 7.1 offers examples of symbols for each of these five categories.

Table 7.1   Possible Symbols

Inviting Style	Meaningful Heritage	School Pride	Academic Excellence	Empowered Staff
Architecture of the building	Displays of past achievements	Mascots	Mission statements	Business cards
Symbol on the door	Halls of honor	Banners	Academic events	Laptops for the staff
Availability of the principal	Awards, trophies, and plaques	Songs	Student work displays	Telephones in the classroom

Inviting Style

One way a school projects an inviting style is in its architecture. Of course, for years schools were built like factories. Some of these factory-like schools are so old that no one would want to be in them. But more and more schools today are expansive and open and thus more inviting. More and more schools exemplify places people enjoy being in. This is especially important in a day when schools are encouraging more parents and more community members to be part of the total life of the school.

There are some very simple ways to embody inviting style. For example, in one large school district with many large schools around the city, it was often difficult to know which door was the public entrance. Consequently, this school district painted an image of the city's flag onto the appropriate entrance, making it easy for a newcomer or a visitor.

Another key symbol that communicates much is the presence of the principal. I realize that every principal has hours and hours of paperwork to get done almost daily. Therefore, I am always impressed when I see the principal walking the halls and talking with teachers and students. By doing this, the principal conveys an inviting, open style that can indeed affect the entire school community.

Bright colors can also communicate a welcoming style. A simple sign welcoming visitors can also help. Some schools have found a room they have labeled the parent or school volunteer room. All of this shows that the school wants teachers, students, parents, and the community to be part of the learning community.

Several schools in a large urban city have created small gardens around them. The plants grow green in the spring. Soon flowers appear. As people walk by those gardens, the school projects an atmosphere of welcome. It projects a commitment to care for surroundings. Consequently, it indirectly communicates their care for each student.

Meaningful Heritage

It is compelling to grasp the notable aspects of a school's past history. Consequently, any displays of past achievements can communicate this easily. This need not just be sports achievements but also academic or service achievements, as well as recognition of well-known and accomplished graduates (authors, politicians, decorated military personnel, actors, etc). Displays of actual awards, plaques, or trophies are other ways that a school's meaningful heritage is celebrated through these very concrete symbols.

School Pride

Symbols are often used to enhance school pride. Very often the school mascot can become a rallying point for school pride (a bulldog, warrior, lion, eagle, etc.). When the characteristics of the mascot are talked about, the mascot symbol becomes more and more effective.

The school song can also be a symbol that enhances school pride. Particularly if the words and music are relevant to the lives of the faculty and students, the song can occasion genuine pride when it is heard or when it is sung.

More and more these days people are hanging colorful, decorative banners in the hallways and classrooms, often with encouraging sayings or praise included on them. They can have a distinct visual impact that serves to increase school pride.

Academic Excellence

The primary task of the school is to encourage and facilitate academic excellence. Very often the school's mission statement supports this. I have visited schools that display the mission statement liberally throughout the school. This then becomes a symbolic reminder to everyone in the learning community of what they are about.

Academic events like debates, spelling bees, and participation in writing contests can also be symbols that point to the primary task of academic excellence. For many high school students, being invited to the National Honor Society is that kind of symbol. Winning scholarships to college can also represent that.

Displays of students' work can also become symbols that communicate academic excellence. When students' work is displayed tastefully and appropriately and is changed periodically, it can become a dramatic way to herald academic excellence.

Empowered Staff

Sometimes simple things can become strong symbols for the staff. One principal made sure that each staff member had business cards to pass out whenever meeting with parents or others in the community. This communicated to the all staff members their importance and their role in the learning community.

Another principal got the financial support for telephones to be put into every classroom. This not only countered the tremendous isolation that many teachers feel, it also allowed the teachers a convenient tool to contact parents right from the classroom. In addition, the telephones made it easy for the office to contact the teacher and the teacher to contact the office.

Some districts have made sure that all of their staff have laptop computers. This conveys not only a general desire to equip staff with tools needed but also communicates that technology and the world of computers are crucial elements for what it means to be a teacher in these districts.

All of the above very physical items carry huge symbolic power. These symbols communicate that in these districts the students and the teachers are "top of the pyramid," so to speak. These symbols communicate that the principal and the district are there to guide and serve the teachers and the students.

ASTUTE LEADERSHIP PAYS ATTENTION TO THE ROLE OF SYMBOLS ■

The effective leader understands the power of symbols. In fact, the effective leader is a symbol. Unconsciousness about the role of symbols and unconsciousness about the leader being a symbol can deprive the leader of powerful tools for building spirit in the school. "Our work has taught us that the symbolic expressive facets of organizational life are at the heart of inspired leadership" (Bolman & Deal, 1995, p. 39). Another way to talk about the role of the leader is that the leader is always paying attention to bringing the meaning and significance of the work to the forefront of consciousness (Bolman & Deal, 2002, p. 118). Unless this is done, the depths of spirit that drive motivation and excellence will be lost to the school.

There are many ways that the leader can pay attention to symbols. Deal and Peterson suggest many ways that school leaders pay attention to symbols and even become symbols themselves. Table 7.2 organizes many

Table 7.2 Leadership as Symbol

Decisive Action	Academic Integrity	Open Communication	Dynamic Collegiality	Meaning Promotion
Willingness to act	Intellectual engagement	Communicator of ideas	Collegial sharing	Event creator
Servant style	Writing skill	Advocacy	Warm greetings	Storyteller
Holder of accountability	Professional learning	Active listener	Joy, laughter, fun	Relevant rituals
"The-buck-stops-here" attitude	Instructional leadership	Consensus generator	Recognition	Use of song and drama

SOURCE: Adapted from Deal, T. E., & Peterson, K. (1999). *Shaping school culture*, pp. 65-167. San Francisco: Jossey-Bass.

of these suggestions into five overarching categories: Decisive Action, Academic Integrity, Open Communication, Dynamic Collegiality, and Meaning Promotion.

Decisive Action

The school leader reveals Decisive Action when he or she demonstrates a definite willingness to act. This means that when the data and situation reveal that action is required, this leader acts. Also, the school leader reveals Decisive Action by carrying out continual servant acts. This means anything from proudly leading school tours to showing up early for professional inservice days and bringing coffee and food or making sure it's available for the staff. Decisive Action also involves being a holder of accountability. This means finding appropriate ways to hold staff and students to the commitments they have made. Finally, Decisive Action includes modeling "the buck stops here." This means taking responsibility for the school and every aspect of its life. It also means admitting to mistakes when the leader has made them.

Academic Integrity

The school leader models Academic Integrity by the leader's ability to engage all of the staff and students in the task of academic excellence. This means that the leader is knowledgeable about educational matters and concerns and facilitates the spread of that knowledge among all the staff. The school leader further shows academic integrity in his or her writing. This means that everything from letters sent to parents and memos sent to teachers to material sent to local newspapers reveals the leader's knowledge, as well as the leader's deep commitment to the mission of the school. Academic Integrity is further revealed through the continual professional learning that the leader engages in as well as the continual professional learning the leader encourages throughout the staff. Finally, instructional leadership shows this academic integrity—one principal spends 80 percent of the time as an instructional leader, visiting classes and coaching teachers. That may be unrealistic for most leaders, but finding a way to do that increases the symbolic power of the leader.

Open Communication

The school leader strengthens the symbolic with open, direct, and honest communication. One dimension of Open Communication is the ability to communicate ideas. This means the ability to convey a vision that attracts support or the ability to elicit from the staff a mission that is both exciting and realistic. Another dimension of Open Communication is advocacy. First and foremost this means advocacy on behalf of the students, that is, keeping student learning and achievement as the top priority of every day. Second, this means advocacy on behalf of the staff. Simply put, even though the school leader may be part of the administration, the staff members experience the principal as being on their side. A third dimension of Open Communication is active listening. Basically, this means that people experience that the school leader has heard what they have said and has acknowledged it in such a way that they know the leader has gotten the point. The final dimension of Open Communication is consensus generation. This is perhaps the most difficult dimension for it requires the school leader to have the skill to enable a group with diverse perspectives to come to agreement on the fundamental underlying aspects of the issue at hand.

Dynamic Collegiality

The school leader increases the symbolic by embodying dynamic, interactive collegiality. One way the school leader does this is through collegial sharing. This not only means that the leader spends a lot of time talking to teachers, parents, support staff, the board, and the community, but also that the leader enables such sharing to occur within and among those constituencies. Another way the school leader conveys this is simply through genuinely warm greetings and conversations. This means that among many other skills, the school leader cultivates people skills. A related but distinct way the school leader does this is by embodying joy, laughter, and fun. The job of a school leader, whether principal, assistant principal, lead teacher, or a teacher of great longevity in the school is overwhelming. One might even say impossible at times. Yet if the school leader is not enjoying the role of leader, the leader will definitely convey misery and sourness to everyone he or she meets. People will dread contact with that leader. When that happens, the leader has lost attention on the symbolic and has lost the symbolic power of the role. Finally, the leader enhances dynamic collegiality by always offering recognition to others rather than pointing the attention to the leader. Celebrating the teacher victories, honoring student achievements, and recognizing the important roles of support staff are all ways the leader can offer recognition to others.

Meaning Promotion

Underlying all of these symbols of leadership is the ability of the school leader to elicit meaning and significance from the often mundane tasks that must be done as part of the overall mission of education. People's morale dies, spirit dies in the midst of no meaning and no significance. But meaning and significance do not just happen. They need to be called forth. They need to be elicited. At times they need to be dragged out of situations.

One way the school leader does this is by occasioning events. People mark time through events. Open House at school, Teacher Appreciation Week, Reading Nights, Career Fairs, and others are all events that point to the meaning of education in a variety of ways. They all take work, but they all pay off when done well. Not only do these motivate the teachers, but such events also motivate the students and the parents.

Another way the school leader promotes meaning is through storytelling. Chapter 5 dealt entirely with the importance of storytelling. If the school leader is not a natural storyteller, he or she should locate the great storytellers among the staff. Stories from the past, stories highlighting classroom successes, and stories featuring student accomplishments all help to generate meaning and significance.

A third way the school leader promotes significance is by fostering relevant rituals and ceremonies (as discussed in Chapter 6). It is the leader's role to make sure that school rituals and ceremonies are high quality and filled with meaning. This is another way that the school leader guards the symbolic.

Finally, the school leader makes use of song and drama. Encouraging teachers and students to write words to a familiar tune about the year coming to a close, or inviting teachers and students to create a short drama about getting ready for the yearly standardized tests, are examples of how a leader might make use of song and drama. Messages can get communicated indirectly in those mediums that more direct mediums can't successfully communicate.

Bolman and Deal (2002, p. 4) lay out four lenses the effective school leader needs to use. They suggest that most school leaders keep the structural (daily schedule, yearly calendar, class scheduling, policies, etc.) lens and the human resource (hiring, classroom observation, teacher teams, etc.) lens close to their awareness. They may not pay close attention to the political (decision-making policies, relationships to the board and the community, connection to the district level) lens or the symbolic (what we've been talking about in the last three chapters) lens, although sometimes the symbolic lens generates the most passion and heat. Think about trying to change the school mascot or school colors. Think about trying to tear down an old school to build a new one. Think about changing the format of the graduation ceremony. Think about not allowing the celebration of holidays that once had religious beginnings. The symbolic generates much passion and much heat.

■ SYMBOLS BIND PEOPLE TOGETHER

Because symbols communicate meaning and significance differently than words do, symbols have a great power to bind people together. They can tie people to the deeper purpose of what education and schooling are all about (Deal & Peterson, 1999, p. 68). Once the meaning and significance of education and schooling have been experienced, appropriate symbols remind people and bring them back to the power of those experiences. Symbols can invite school pride. As stated above, try changing them or monkeying around with them and see what passions get aroused. Appropriate and relevant symbols touch the very core of human beings. They connect very directly with peoples' deep beliefs.

ACTIVITY THIRTY-FOUR—STRENGTHEN SCHOOL CULTURE WITH VISUAL SYMBOLS ■

Description

Schools have used the impact of visual symbols when designating school colors and school mascots. These come into play most frequently in sports venues. These colors and symbols channel a great deal of energy during sports games and pep rallies. Visual symbols related to the primary mission of the school can also generate energy and motivation for the learning task. For the symbols to have the most power, it is crucial for everyone not only to understand what the symbols mean but also to be able to talk about the symbols—to tell the stories behind the symbols.

Methodology

1. Discern the hallmarks or unique qualities of the school or class.
2. Write them on chart paper so that all can see them.
3. Use qualities of powerful symbols: visually catching, simple, clear.
4. Provide chart paper and magic markers.
5. Divide the group into teams.
6. Have each team create a symbol suggestion.
7. When completed, ask each team to share theirs.
8. Note any similarities among the elements in the symbols.
9. From these similarities have the group build their one symbol.

Example

Figure 7.2 shows St. Anne Catholic School's Anniversary symbol.

The symbol with the diamond came from St. Anne's Catholic School for their 75th anniversary celebration. The diamond communicated to them that their school and the quality of education they provided would last forever. This was a simple image yet communicated a great deal.

Figure 7.2   St. Anne Catholic School's Anniversary Symbol

75 years and still shining.

Figure 7.3 shows the Chicago Reading Initiative symbol.

Figure 7.3   Chicago Reading Initiative Symbol

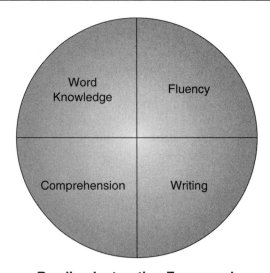

Reading Instruction Framework
Chicago Reading Initiative

The Chicago Reading Initiative symbol is again simple, yet it conveys the four essentials that Chicago Public Schools emphasized in their work on literacy with local schools. Very large representations of this symbol were hung in school libraries, so the symbol greets all the students and teachers as they spend time in the library.

Figure 7.4 shows the Strategic Learning Lens symbol.

Figure 7.4   Strategic Learning Lens Symbol

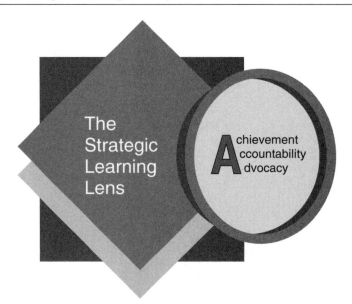

The Academy for Urban School Leaders

The Strategic Learning Lens symbol was created for a summer academy. The major themes of the summer were clearly communicated with the three A's: Achievement, Accountability, and Advocacy.

Metacognitive Insights

Part of the power of symbols is the process used to create them, including the dialogue that occurs during the creation. What happens with these symbols is also crucial. They need to appear all over the school. Teachers and students need to talk about them. Conversations can occur linking happenings in the life of the school with the symbols. For example, a whole-school event or a class can dramatize what we are about and what the symbol is about. Very often such symbols can communicate more than just words.

ACTIVITY THIRTY-FIVE—ENHANCE THE ARTS   ■

Description

As Howard Gardner's theory of multiple intelligences suggests and schools like the Key School in Indianapolis have verified, students come alive when their intelligence gifts are used in school. There are others who suggest that involvement in the arts such as drama, music, art, and dance actually enhances academic performance. The arts have a way of tapping into deep motivation, and increasing students' motivation can increase their desire to learn and achieve. While this information supports arts programs, many schools, for budgetary reasons, have had to eliminate most if not all programs in the arts. So how can the classroom promote the arts without arts programs? This is where the theory of multiple intelligences and the related theory of differentiated instruction enter in. Each classroom can use the arts to help teach curriculum content. Using the screen of multiple intelligences, there are several ways to bring the arts into the classroom no matter what the subject.

Methodology

1. *Verbal/Linguistic*—Writing and acting out plays, use of mnemonics

2. *Logical/Mathematical*—Creating graphs to illustrate history or social studies information; ways to see the mathematical influence in music

3. *Visual/Spatial*—Use of graphic organizers, creating pictures of concepts

4. *Bodily/Kinesthetic*—Building models for scientific study; building historical models; acting out vocabulary words

5. *Musical/Rhythmic*—Listening to music from historical periods; writing music or words to familiar melodies to teach concepts

6. *Interpersonal*—Cooperative group presentations involving visuals; creating group skits or short dramas connected to the curriculum

7. *Intrapersonal*—Individual poetry writing; individual collages illustrating a literary theme

8. *Naturalist*—Artistic representation of scientific themes or concepts; artistic creation of natural materials (leaves, grasses, dried flowers, etc.).

Example

Teachers have had students rewrite a scene from a Shakespeare play with contemporary characters and story. Then the students act out the drama in the classroom. Teachers have had students put mathematical concepts and principles into rap music. Teachers have had students study the art of a historical period. Teachers have had students pantomime words and concepts. Teachers of elementary students have had their students write, illustrate, and then publish their own books.

Several schools I know of feature famous art work on the walls. One such school even has their students try to copy the artwork, thus learning the technique the artist used.

Metacognitive Insights

I can't emphasize enough the power of the arts to raise the morale of students and to call forth their motivation. Sometimes it is only the arts that speak to the depths of emotions students are experiencing. Furthermore, some students can only reveal these emotional depths by participating in the arts. Needless to say, all this does a great deal for the staff, too.

■ ACTIVITY THIRTY-SIX—ENCOURAGE TEAM/COOPERATIVE GROUP SYMBOLS

Description

Creating a team or cooperative group symbol is a way of binding a group together, a way of cementing its identity and its purpose. A symbol is visual. Consequently, the symbol is some kind of graphic. Sometimes it is possible to jog a team's thinking by asking it to create its own flag. Or one might catalyze creativity by getting team members to create a T-shirt design. The dialogue that occurs among team members as they create the design contributes to the powerful message of the resulting product.

Methodology

1. Have a group or team ask itself who the team members are. What are the gifts of the members?

2. Have the group or team ask itself what its purpose, task, or goal is. What is it out to accomplish? Why have the members formed as a team or a group?

3. Looking at the results of their brainstorming, have the team discern some of its unique qualities—either in task or in team makeup.

4. Think of particular shapes such as a circle, a triangle, a square, or a pentagon.

5. Attach the elements of the essence of the team to the chosen shape.

6. Embellish the symbol in any appropriate way.

Example

A high school social studies team studying the middle ages might decide that their chief image was *Knights on a Quest*, and create a symbol to depict their image (Figure 7.5).

Figure 7.5 Team Symbol Example

DETERMINATION

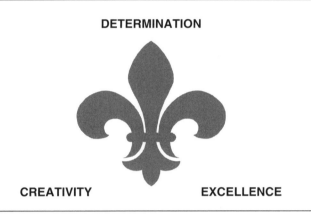

CREATIVITY   **EXCELLENCE**

This symbol illustrates the values they felt were tied to the work they were doing on their middle ages project. Determination indicates they were not going to give up during their research and writing. Creativity indicates they were going to make their project and presentation imaginative and attractive. Finally, excellence indicates the quality they were after in their work.

Metacognitive Insights

During the carrying out of a team's task, viewing its symbol becomes a reminder of what the team is about. For the middle ages project team members, when the research and preparation begin to get overwhelming, just looking at the symbol can bring back the entire conversation they had creating it. It can bring back their motivation to model determination, creativity, and excellence.

IN CLOSING ■

I anticipate that the tools described in this book will inspire even more tools for building spirit in learning communities. If we take seriously this challenge to build spirit, my hope is that learning communities will become a significant life force in the entire community. My hope is that learning communities will become a center for much healing in the midst of such divisiveness in our society. Finally, my hope is that teachers will regain the honored status that teachers have held through the ages, the status of bringing new life over and over again both to individuals and to society.

Templates

Template 1 Year's Planned Accomplishments by School Quarters

Quarter / Strategy				

Template 2   Implementation Steps

Accomplishment	What	Who	When

Template 3   Peer Observation Form

OBSERVEE		DATE
SCHOOL		
LESSON FOCUS		
FOCUS OF OBSERVATION		
OBSERVER		
FEEDBACK		
COMMENTS FROM OBSERVEE		
PROPOSED STRATEGIES FOR FUTURE LESSONS		

Template 4   Preobservation Visit Form

Preobservation Visit	
Focus	
Observation tools	
Logistics: Time, where to sit	
Class data	
Lesson plan	
Postobservation visit time	
Observation Notes	

Template 5   Mentor Observation Form

OBSERVEE		DATE:
SCHOOL		
LESSON FOCUS		
FOCUS OF OBSERVATION		
OBSERVER		
FEEDBACK		
COMMENTS FROM OBSERVEE		
PROPOSED STRATEGIES FOR FUTURE LESSONS		

Template 6   Observation Notes

Mentor: _____   Date: _____

Mentee: _____   Class/Grade:_____

I saw . . .

I heard . . .

I thought . . .

Template 7 Cardstorming Chart Form

Template 8 Planning Visible Achievements

Quarter	One	Two	Three	Four
Strategy one				
Strategy two				

Template 9   Portfolio Item Selection Tool

Item Selection Tool
Portfolio Focus:
Personal Professional Development Goal:

Date	Item	Reason For Inclusion

Template 10 Data Screen

Education Indicators	Economic Indicators

Home Life Indicators

Community Life Indicators	Employment Indicators

Template 11 Resource Analysis

Source _____	
Author's insights	
Reflections	
Questions	

Template 12 Training Session Plan

Context	
Need	
Direct teaching	
Actual practice	
Monitoring	
Follow-up plan	
Processing	

Template 13 Conversation Flowchart

Conversation on:

OPENING

OBJECTIVE	REFLECTIVE

INTERPRETIVE	DECISIONAL

CLOSING

Template 14 Staff Meeting Planning Form

Agenda With Key Focus for the Meeting
Icebreaker in Dyads or Triads
Sharing Strategies That Are Working
Focus Item: A Study or a Participatory Workshop
Committee Reports and Announcements
Closing

Bibliography

Adams, J. D. (Ed.). (1986). *Transforming leadership*. Alexandria, VA: Miles River.

Adams, J. D. (Ed.). (1984). *Transforming work*. Alexandria, VA: Miles River.

Astuto, T., Clark, D. L., Read, A., McGree, K., & Fernandez, L. P. (1994). *Roots of reform: Challenging the assumptions that control change in education*. Bloomington, IN: Phi Delta Kappa Educational Foundation.

Azzara, J. R. (2000, December/2001, January). The heart of school leadership. *Educational Leadership, 58*(4), 62–64.

Barbknecht, A., & Kieffer, C. W. (2001). *Peer coaching: The learning team approach*. Arlington Heights, IL: SkyLight.

Barton, E. A. (2000). *Leadership strategies for safe schools*. Arlington Heights, IL: SkyLight.

Bellanca, J. (1995). *Designing professional development for change*. Palatine, IL: IRI/SkyLight.

Bernhardt, V. L. (2000, Winter). Intersections. *Journal of Staff Development, 21*(1), 33–36.

Black, S. (2001, Fall). Child or widget. *Journal of Staff Development, 22*(4), 10–13.

Black, S. (2003, Summer). Try, try again. *Journal of Staff Development, 24*(3), 12–17.

Blake, R. R., Mouton, J. S., & Allen, R. L. (1987). *Spectacular teamwork*. New York: John Wiley.

Bolman, L. G., & Deal, T. E. (1995). *Leading with soul*. San Francisco: Jossey-Bass.

Bolman, L. G., & Deal, T. E. (2002). *Reframing the path to school leadership*. Thousand Oaks, CA: Corwin.

Brandt, R. (2002). The case for diversified schooling. *Educational Leadership, 59*(7), 12–19.

Burke, K. (Ed.). (1992). *Authentic assessment: A collection*. Palatine, IL: IRI/SkyLight.

Burke, K. (1997). *Designing professional portfolios for change*. Arlington Heights, IL: IRI/SkyLight.

Burke, K. (1999). *The mindful school: How to assess authentic learning* (3rd ed.). Arlington Heights, IL: SkyLight.

Burke, K., Fogarty, R., & Belgrad, S. (2002). *The portfolio connection* (2nd ed.). Arlington Heights, IL: SkyLight.

Burke, K. (Ed.). (1996). *Professional portfolios.* Arlington Heights, IL: IRI/SkyLight.

Byham, W. C. (1992). *Zapp! In education.* New York: Fawcett Columbine.

Caine, R. N., & Caine, G. (1997). *Education on the edge of possibility.* Alexandria, VA: Association for Supervision and Curriculum Development.

Caine, R. N., & Caine, G. (1991). *Making connections: Teaching and the human brain.* Alexandria, VA: Association for Supervision and Curriculum Development.

Caine, G., Caine, R. N., & Crowell, S. (1994). *Mindshifts: A brain-based process for restructuring schools and renewing education.* Tucson, AZ: Zephyr.

Cohen, P. (1995). Understanding the brain. *Educational Leadership, 37*(7), 1–5.

Costa, A. L. (1991). *The school as home for the mind.* Palatine, IL: SkyLight.

Covey, S. R. (1989). *The 7 habits of highly effective people.* New York: Simon & Schuster.

DeForest, C. (1986). The art of conscious celebration: A new concept for today's leaders. In J. Adams (Ed.), *Transforming leadership* (pp. 221–231). Alexandria, VA: Miles River.

Deal, T. E., & Peterson, K. (1999). *Shaping school culture.* San Francisco: Jossey-Bass.

Dicembre, E. (2002, Spring). How they turned the ship around. *Journal of Staff Development, 23*(2), 32–35.

Dickman, M. H., & Stanford-Blair, N. (2002). *Connecting leadership to the brain.* Thousand Oaks, CA: Corwin.

Dietz, M. E. (2001). *Designing the school leader's portfolio.* Arlington Heights, IL: SkyLight.

DuFour, R. (2000, Winter). Data put a face on shared vision. *Journal of Staff Development, 21*(1), 71–72.

Eoyang, G. H. (1997). *Coping with chaos.* Cheyenne, WY: Lagumo.

Fogarty, R. (1995). *Best practices for the learner-centered classroom.* Palatine, IL: IRI/SkyLight.

Fogarty, R. (Ed.). (1996). *Student portfolios.* Arlington Heights, IL: IRI/SkyLight.

Fogarty, R. (1997). *Brain compatible classrooms.* Arlington Heights, IL: SkyLight.

Fogarty, R. (1997). *Problem-based learning and other curriculum models for the multiple intelligences.* Arlington Heights, IL: IRI/SkyLight.

Fullan, M. (1993). *Change forces: Probing the depths of educational reform.* New York: Falmer.

Fullan, M. G., & Stiegelbauer, S. (1991). *The meaning of educational change.* New York: Teachers College, Columbia University.

Fullan, M., & Hargreaves, A. (1996). *What's worth fighting for in your school.* New York: Teachers College, Columbia University.

Ganser, T. (2000, Winter). Teams of two. *Journal of Staff Development, 21*(1), 60–63.

Gardner, H. (1994). Educating for understanding. *Phi Delta Kappan, 75*(7), 563–565.

Gardner, H. (1995). The theory of multiple intelligences. In R. Fogarty & J. Bellanca (Eds.), *Multiple intelligences: A collection* (pp. 82–99). Palatine, IL: IRI/SkyLight.

Gardner, H. (1996, Spring). Your child's intelligence(s). *Scholastic Parent & Child,* 32–37.

Gardner, H. (2000). *The disciplined mind.* New York: Penguin.

Gideon, B. H., & Erlandson, D. A. (2001, Fall). Here's what happens when the principal says "I want you to come up with the ideas." *Journal of Staff Development, 22*(4), 14–17.

Glasser, W. (1986). *Control theory in the classroom.* New York: Perennial Library, Harper & Row.

Glasser, W. (1990). *The quality school.* New York: Perennial Library, Harper & Row.

Glickman, C. D. (2002). *Leadership for learning.* Alexandria, VA: Association of Supervision and Curriculum Development.

Goleman, D. (1995). *Emotional intelligence.* New York: Bantam.

Gottesman, B. (2000). *Peer coaching for educators.* Lanham, MD: Scarecrow.

Hansel, L., Huie, D., & Martinez, M. (2002, Spring). Same view of the landscape. *Journal of Staff Development, 23*(2), 36–39.

Harris, P. (Ed.). (1994). *Violence and the schools.* Palatine, IL: IRI/SkyLight.

Hoffman, D., & Levak, B. A. (2003, September). Personalizing schools. *Educational Leadership, 61*(1), 30–34.

Idol, L. (1997). *Creating collaborative and inclusive schools.* Austin, TX: Eitel.

Jason, M. H. (2003). *Evaluating programs to increase student achievement.* Glenview, IL: SkyLight.

Jaworski, J. (1996). *Synchronicity: The inner path of leadership.* San Francisco: Berrett-Koehler.

Jenlink, P. (Ed.). 1995. *Systemic change: Touchstone for the future school.* Palatine, IL: IRI/SkyLight.

Johnson, S. M., & Birkeland, S. E. (2003, May). The schools that teachers choose. *Educational Leadership, 60*(8), 20–24.

Joyce, B., & Showers, B. (1995). *Student achievement through staff development* (2nd ed.). White Plains, NY: Longman.

Joyce, B., Wolf, J., & Calhoun, E. (1993). *The self-renewing school.* Alexandria, VA: Association of Supervisors and Curriculum Development.

Kohn, A. (1986). *No contest.* Boston: Houghton Mifflin.

Kohn, A. (1990). *The brighter side of human nature.* New York: Basic Books.

Kriete, R. (2003, September). Start the day with community. *Educational Leadership, 61*(1), 68–70.

LeDoux, J. (1996). *The emotional brain: The mysterious underpinnings of emotional life.* New York: Simon & Schuster.

LeTendre, B. G. (2000, Winter). Six steps to a solution. *Journal of Staff Development, 21*(1), 20–25.

Lewellen, J. R. (1994). *A parents' guide to quality schools.* New York: Vantage.

Marshak, D. (1997). *Action research on block scheduling.* Larchmont, NY: Eye On Education.

Marzano, R. J. (2003). *What works in schools.* Alexandria, VA: Association for Supervision and Curriculum Development.

Marzano, R. J., Marzano, J. S., & Pickering, D. J. (2003). *Classroom management that works.* Alexandria, VA: Association for Supervision and Curriculum Development.

Marzano, R. J., Pickering, D. J., & Pollock, J. E. (2001). *Classroom instruction that works.* Alexandria, VA: Association for Supervision and Curriculum Development.

McCormick, J. H. (2002). *The professional growth plan: A school leader's guide to the process.* Arlington Heights, IL: SkyLight.

Mendes, E. (2003, September). What empathy can do? *Educational Leadership, 61*(1), 56–59.

Miles, K. H. (2003, Summer). The big picture. *Journal of Staff Development, 24*(3), 34–37.

Moir, E., & Bloom, G. (2003, May). Fostering leadership through mentoring. *Educational Leadership, 60*(8), 58–60.

Nelson, J. (2001). *The art of focused conversation for schools.* Gabriola Island, BC, Canada: New Society.

Nevills, P. (Winter, 2003). Cruising the cerebral superhighway. *Journal of Staff Development, 24*(1), 20–23.

Newberry, A. J. H. (1992). *Strategic planning in education.* Vancouver, BC, Canada: EduServ.

Nieto, S. M. (2003, May). What keeps teachers going? *Educational Leadership, 60*(8), 14–18.

Owen, H. (1987). *Spirit: Transformation and development in organizations.* Potomac, MD: Abbott.

Palmer, P. (1998). *The courage to teach.* San Francisco: Jossey-Bass.

Pardini, P. (2000, Winter). Data, well done. *Journal of Staff Development, 21*(1), 12–18.

Parry, T., & Gregory, G. (1998). *Designing brain-compatible learning.* Arlington Heights, IL: SkyLight.

Peine, J. M. (2003, Winter). Planning, measuring their own growth. *Journal of Staff Development, 24*(1), 38–42.

Pete, B. M., & Sambo, C. S. (2004). Data, dialogue, and decisions. In R. Fogarty & B. Pete (Eds.), *Teaching and learning: An anthology for professional teachers.* Chicago: Robin Fogarty & Associates.

Pitton, D. E. (2000). *Mentoring novice teachers.* Arlington Heights, IL: SkyLight.

Riggs, E. G., & Gholar, C. R. (2004). *Connecting with students' will to succeed: The power of conation.* Glenview, IL: Pearson.

Salzman, J. (2002). *The promise of mentoring.* Chicago: Robin Fogarty & Associates.

Sargent, B. (2003, May). Finding good teachers—and keeping them. *Educational Leadership, 60*(8), 44–47.

Saphier, J., & D'Auria J. (1993). *How to bring vision to school improvement.* Carlisle, MA: Research for Better Teaching.

Scherer, M. (2002, September). Do students care about learning? A conversation with Mihaly Csikszentmihalyi. *Educational Leadership, 60*(1), 12–17.

Schmoker, M. (2001). *The results fieldbook.* Alexandria, VA: Association for Supervision and Curriculum Development.

Schmuck, R. A., & Miles, M. B. (1971). *Organization development in schools.* La Jolla, CA: University Associates.

Schrenko, L. (1994). *Structuring a learner-centered school.* Palatine, IL: IRI/SkyLight.

Senge, P. (1990). *The fifth discipline*. New York: Doubleday.

Senge, P., Kleiner, A., Roberts, C., Ross, R. B., & Smith, R. J. (1994). *The fifth discipline fieldbook*. New York: Doubleday.

Siegel, J., & Shaughnessy, M. F. (1994). Educating for understanding: An interview with Howard Gardner. *Phi Delta Kappan, 75*(7), 563–565.

Smith, G. A. (2002, September). Going local. *Educational Leadership, 60*(1), 30–33.

Sparks, D. (2003, Winter). Change agent. *Journal of Staff Development, 24*(1), 55–58.

Sparks, D. (2003, Summer). Honor the human heart. *Journal of Staff Development, 24*(3), 49–53.

Sparks, D. (2003, Spring). The answer to "when?" is "now." *Journal of Staff Development, 24*(2), 52–55.

Sparks, D. (2003, Fall). We care, therefore they learn. *Journal of Staff Development, 24*(4), 42–47.

Spencer, L. (1989). *Winning through participation*, Dubuque, IA: Kendall/Hunt.

Stanfield, R. B. (Ed.). (1997). *The art of focused conversation*, Toronto, ON, Canada: The Canadian Institute of Cultural Affairs.

Stanfield, R. B. (2000). *The courage to lead*, Gabriola Island, BC, Canada: New Society Publishers.

Strong, R., Silver, H., Perini, M., & Tuculescu, G. (2003, September). Boredom and its opposite. *Educational Leadership, 61*(1), 24–29.

Sylwester, R. (1995). *A celebration of neurons: An educator's guide to the human brain*. Alexandria, VA: Association for Supervision and Curriculum Development.

Troxel, J. P. (Ed.). (1993). *Participation works: Business cases from around the world*. Alexandria, VA: Miles River.

Wellman, B., & Lipton, L. (2000, Winter). Navigation. *Journal of Staff Development, 21*(1), 47–50.

Wheatley, M. J. (1992). *Leadership and the new science*, San Francisco: Berrett-Koehler.

Williams, D. T. (2003, November). Rural routes to success. *Educational Leadership, 61*(3), 66–70.

Williams, J. S. (2003, May). Why great teachers stay. *Educational Leadership, 60*(8). 71–74.

Williams, R. B. (1993). *More than 50 ways to build team consensus*, Arlington Heights, IL: IRI/SkyLight.

Williams, R. B. (1997). *Twelve roles of facilitators of school change*, Arlington Heights, IL: IRI/SkyLight.

Wolk, S. (2003, September). Hearts and minds. *Educational Leadership, 61*(1), 14–18.

Wyatt, L. D. (1996, September). More time, more training. *The School Administrator, 53*(8), 16–18.

Index

**CORWIN
PRESS**

The Corwin Press logo—a raven striding across an open book—represents the union of courage and learning. Corwin Press is committed to improving education for all learners by publishing books and other professional development resources for those serving the field of PreK–12 education. By providing practical, hands-on materials, Corwin Press continues to carry out the promise of its motto: **"Helping Educators Do Their Work Better."**